INSPIRI
EDUCATIO
FUN FACTS
FOR KIDS
WITH
COMIC + JOKES

CW01653507

New Fascinating Graphical Science Book for kids 7-14

CURIOUS ROOBI

Knowledge
Is
Power

© Copyright 2021 by Curious Roobi

All rights reserved

No part of this book may be reproduced or used in any manner without the prior written permission of the copyright owner. Please note the information contained within this document is for educational and entertainment purposes only.

Disclaimer Notice :

By reading this document, the reader agrees that under no circumstances is the author responsible for any losses, direct or indirect, that are incurred as a result of the use of the information contained within this document, including, but not limited to, errors, omissions, or inaccuracies. All effort has been executed to present accurate, up-to-date, reliable, complete information.

Legal notice :

This book and all the illustrations in it are copyright protected. It is only for personal use and may not be re-sold or given away to other people. If you would like to share this book with another person, please purchase an additional copy for each person you share it with. No part of this publication may be reproduced, distributed, or transmitted in any form or by any means, including photocopying, recording, or other electronic or mechanical methods, without the prior written permission of the publisher. The content within this book has been derived from various sources. Please consult a licensed professional before attempting any techniques outlined in this book.

ISBN 978-1-7780064-2-5
ISBN 978-1-7780064-0-1
ISBN 978-1-7780064-1-8

For easy access, you can click here or scan the code with your phone

Table of contents

Table of contents

Table of contents

A Special Gift to Our Readers

Included with the purchase of this book is our creativity guide. This guide will help you to avoid making the same mistakes that most parents make which results in losing 98% of kids' creativity by adulthood.

For easy access, you can scan the code with your phone or click the link below.

www.curiousroobi.com

CHAPTER 1: SPACE

Space is a beautiful, mysterious place. It has billions and billions of stars, mysterious moons, galaxies, comets, and other objects and forms of life that are yet to be explored. The sheer vastness of space is beyond human understanding or exhaustive explanation.

We've always known volcanoes to be hot, but can you believe that scientists recently discovered **ice-spewing volcanoes** on **Pluto**? Even more surprising is the fact that Mars has a **massive canyon** as **big as the United States**.

What if there is a giant planet beyond Neptune yet to be discovered? The possibilities are endless, no doubt.

Our knowledge of space is a process that will always be in constant evolution. However, scientists and astronauts have also discovered some really cool facts about space. Read on to learn incredible, fascinating facts, stellar details, and mind-blowing elements about planets, our galaxy, space, and the solar system.

But before some cool facts about space, let's learn a couple of cool terms that you can tell your friends about first.

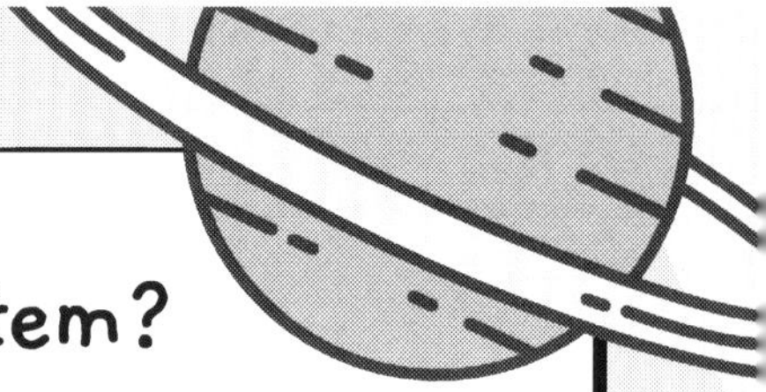

What is the Solar System?

The solar system is built of the sun and all the things that revolve around it. A force called gravity makes it possible for the eight large planets, dwarf planets, asteroids, and comets to move around the sun all year round.

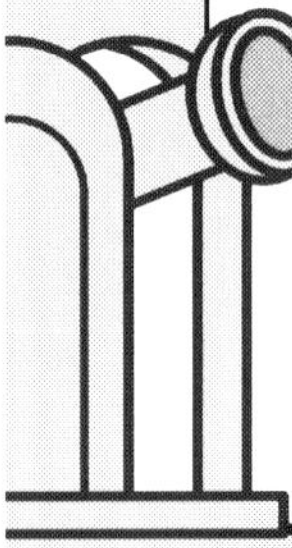

FUN TIME!

Anthony. Why are you standing in the sun? You must be boiling.
I am waiting for my sweat to dry.

What is Space?

Space is the outer atmosphere starting **100 km above** the **Earth**. It is a complete vacuum with **no air or light**. People assume that space is completely empty, but this is untrue. It looks like a pitch-black blanket dotted with millions of stars. Gas and dust can be found in between the planets and stars. Space has harmful ultraviolet and infrared radiation coming from the sun. Star systems nearby also release gamma, cosmic, and energy X-rays that are dangerous to astronauts.

FUN TIME!

An astronaut was in a busy department store but decided to leave. Why?
There was not enough space.

What is our Galaxy?

Our **galaxy** comprises **solar systems**, trillions of stars, and a massive collection of dust and gas held in place by gravitational force. Our planet is called **Earth**, and it exists in the **Milky Way Galaxy**. Gravity holds the Milky Way in space and has a **massive black hole** at its **center**.

The stars you see at night are in our galaxy, the Milky Way. You can see dust bands in the Milky Way at night when you are far away from the pollution of city lights. The **Milky Way is spiral,** but astronauts have discovered other galaxies depending on their shape: **Irregular**, **Elliptical**, and Barred spiral galaxies.

Galaxies collide every once in a while. Due to the vast spaces between them, the stars within each galaxy will move into the spaces in between. New stars will be formed when dust and clouds interact. The galaxies can be pulled into new shapes by gravity to form tails, rings, ellipticals, or even bars.
Now, let us explore some fun facts.

Facts About The Milky Way Galaxy, Planets, & Space

1. The **Sun** is as big as a **million of the Earth's size**, yet scientists still consider it an **average-sized star**. The Sun is just a single star among billions of others in our galaxy.

2. The Sun's visible atmosphere is called the **photosphere**, and it is super hot – the temperatures reach approximately **10,000 degrees Fahrenheit** (5,505 Celsius). However, the atmosphere above the photosphere has temperatures of millions of degrees. Scientists have little to no explanation about this temperature difference between the Sun's surface and the surface above it.

FUN TIME!

Do you know why the sun is always shouting angrily at the clouds?
Because the clouds are always keeping the sun in the shade.

3. It would take you more than **800 years** (8 centuries) to fly from Earth to **Pluto**, the **farthest planet** in our galaxy.

4. Planet **Earth** has more trees than the number of stars in our galaxy. For example, the **Milky Way** has approximately **400 billion stars**, while Earth has about three trillion trees.

5. A day in **Venus** is equal to **243 Earth days**. The **axis** rotation on Venus is so **slow** we are almost three-quarters into the year before a single day ends in Venus.

6. The **Sun** might be **93 million miles** (149,668,992 kilometers) from the Earth, but it only takes **8 minutes** for the **light** to travel from the Sun to the Earth. So that's super-fast, right?

7. It would take **Usain Bolt**, running at full speed, approximately **one year** to get to the **Moon**, Earth's nearest astronomical body.

8. **Proxima Centauri** is the **closest star** to Earth after the sun. However, this star is smaller, colder, and less bright. With a distance of up to **24 trillion miles** from the Earth, it takes approximately four years for its light to reach the Earth.

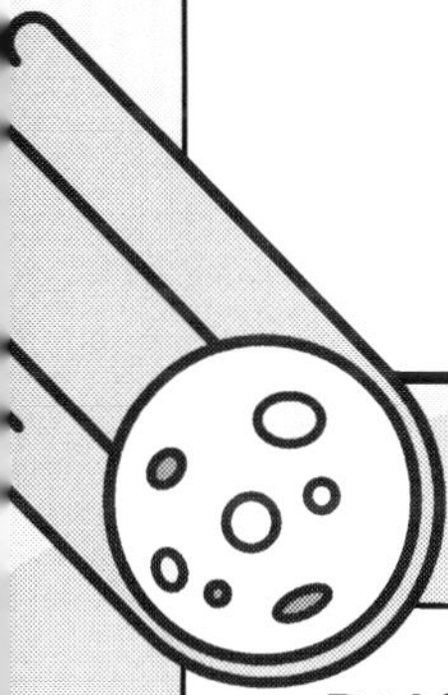

FUN TIME!

If the Sun goes to a fun park, what ride does it always go on first?

The solar coaster

9. Did you know that a **shooting star** isn't a star? It is actually a **meteorite** moving swiftly across the surface of the Earth with gases so hot it glows in the dark.

10. The planet **Jupiter** is gigantic. Planet Earth could fit **1,321 times inside of Jupiter**. In fact, a storm the size of planet Earth has been blowing on Jupiter for hundreds of years. Scientists named this storm the "**Great Red Spot**".

FUN TIME!

All the planets are at a wedding. How do you know that Jupiter, Saturn, Uranus, and Neptune are the ones getting married?

They are all wearing rings.

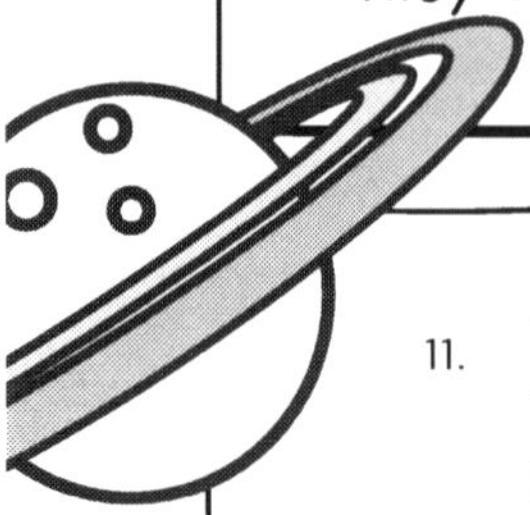

11. The **Milky Way** is a **spiral** with a diameter of approximately 120,000 light-years with over 400 billion stars and probably as many planets.

12. Did you know that **elliptical galaxies** are believed to be older than **spiral galaxies**? That's because scientists have observed that as the burning of gas and dust on spiral galaxies slows down, they slowly lose their shape and become elliptical.

13. Scientists consider **asteroids** and comets "**leftovers**". Not the leftovers for you to eat but the remains of what the solar system used to be.

14. **Galaxies** that create millions of **new stars** at a quick pace are called **Starbursts**. This phenomenon usually occurs when two galaxies merge. This results in the creation of a lot of molecular clouds.

FUN TIME!

Which stars will you see out shopping for sunglasses?

Movie stars.

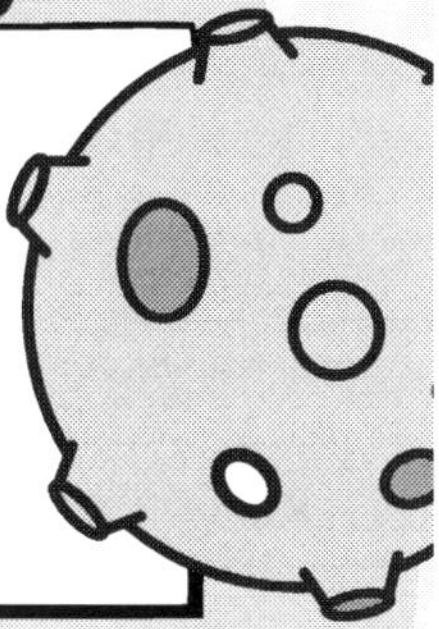

15. **All planets**, except Earth, were named after **Greek and Roman gods**. Earth means "ground" in ancient German English.

16. One of the **largest** objects in **asteroid belt**s is an asteroid called **Vesta**. It is three times the size of Everest (around 22 kilometers).

17. **Stars** are made of hot burning gases. They are mainly composed of **Hydroghydrogenen** gas.

18. The **Earth** has **orbited** the **Milky Way** approximately **18 times** since it was formed, making our planet **18 galactic years old**. The solar system revolves around the galaxy only once in 250 years.

FUN TIME!

I was so proud of myself when I reached the summit of Mount Everest, but my friend pointed out that everything would go downhill from that point.

FUN TIME!

For years, I wondered what the difference between the Sun and the Earth was.

It was just the word "and".

1

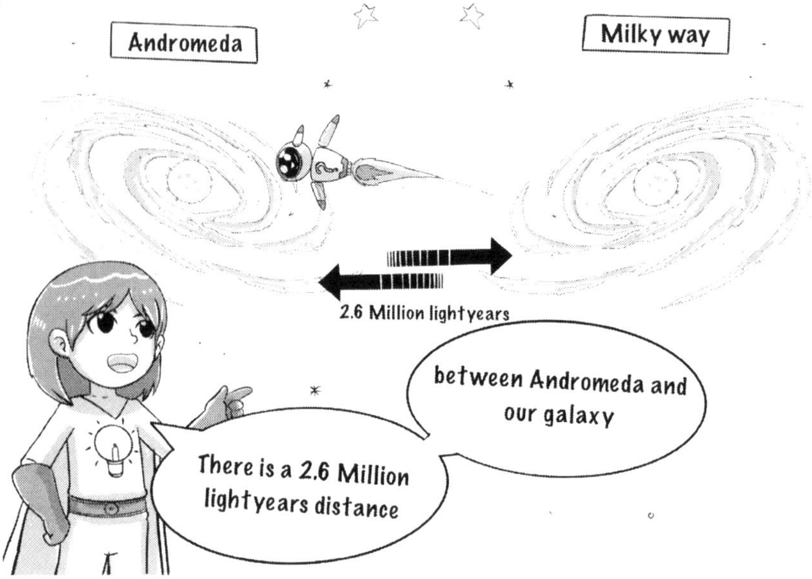

19. **Andromeda** is the galaxy **closest** to the Milky Way, and it is approximately **2.6 million light-years** away from our galaxy.

20. **Pluto** is **no longer** considered part of the **nine planets**. The International Astronomical Unit renamed it in August 2006 because it didn't meet all the criteria needed to be classified as a planet. Pluto is referred to as a **dwarf planet** now.

21. Did you know sometimes a **total solar eclipse** makes **animals** a little **confused**, making them behave strangely?

FUN TIME!

Why was the sun happy on the day of a solar eclipse? Because it had a day off.

22. **Five billion tons** of mass are **lost** from the Sun **every hour** if a **solar wind** occurs on its surface.

23. The observable **universe** alone could have **170 billion galaxies**. Some galaxies are so huge they contain at least one trillion stars, while others are small, with a maximum of around 10 million stars.

24. Microscopic animals called **tardigrades** have survived the cold, airless atmosphere in space. They were sent back into Earth's orbit, where they survived and came back alive. Human beings would die in a matter of seconds if they landed in space without protective space suits or spaceships.

25. Scientists estimate that most **galaxies** could be **100,000 light-years** across in the distance.

26. The **largest** galaxy in this group is the **Andromeda Galaxy**, followed by our **Milky Way** and the **Triangulum** Galaxy. There could be at least **30 other galaxies** in our local group.

27. We have **181 moons** in our **Solar System,** along with eight major and five dwarf planets, 3083 comets, and 552,894 asteroids.

FUN TIME!

Boy: Mom, when you said there is a full moon outside, does that mean it has had enough to eat?

28. **Space** has **no atmosphere**, which means no medium exists. So sound can not travel there, which means that space is pitch black and completely silent. So the only way astronauts can communicate is through radio because waves and frequencies can still be received and sent.

29. Every **planet** in the Solar system has **unique** characteristics. For example, Jupiter is made up of gas, while Earth is made of rock.

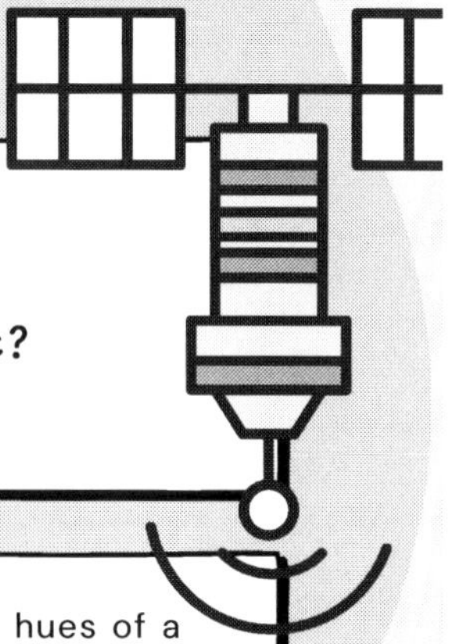

FUN TIME!

Where would you go in space to hear great music?
Nep tunes

30. Everyone loves the golden (orange, yellow, and red) hues of a beautiful **sunset**, but the sunset on **Mars** comes across as **blue**.

31. The planet **Saturn** is famously known for its **rings** made of frozen water particles (ice).

FUN TIME!

What should we do when Saturn is lonely?
Give it a ring sometimes.

32. The universe has more stars than all the **sand** in every single beach in the world combined. Scientists estimate that there are at least **one billion trillion** stars in the universe. It's safer to say that **no one knows** how many stars genuinely exist.

33. Jupiter, Neptune, Saturn, Uranus have **no solid matter**. So you wouldn't be **able to walk on** them as you do here on Earth.

34. The **Sun** is so **heavy**; its mass takes up approximately **99.86%**of all the weight in our solar system.

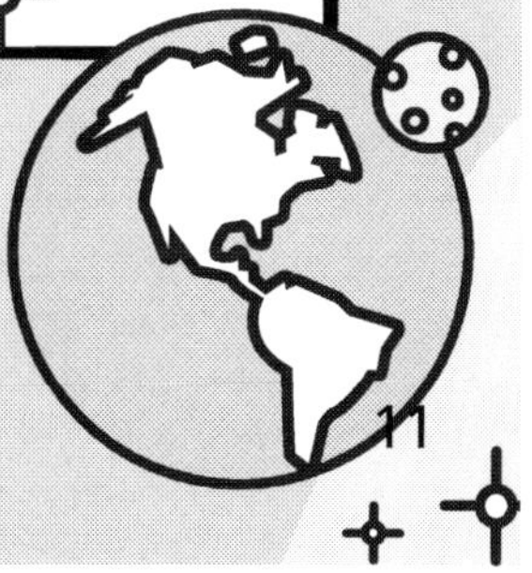

FUN TIME!

For what reason did the Sun decide to start attending school?

It wanted to become brighter.

35. Scientists discovered a **planet made of diamonds.** The planet is called **55 Cancri e**, and it is twice the size of Earth and eight times its weight. We would all be wealthy if we paid just one visit to this mysterious planet.

36. The **footprints** left by **Apollo astronauts** on the **moon** will stay there for millions if not billions of years. That's because the moon has **no wind** that could blow dust over the prints or even water that could wash over them.

FUN TIME!

Why do restaurants on the Moon have no customers?

Because they lack atmosphere.

37. Space has **floating water**. Scientists discovered the mass of floating water vapor is approximately **140 trillion times** the weight of **water on Earth's** water bodies combined.

38. We would be **baked alive on Venus,** the hottest planet with a temperature of **460 degrees Celsius**. But, on the other hand, we would **freeze to death** in **Uranus**, the coldest planet. Its average temperature is **-220 degrees Celsius.**

FUN TIME!

Q: Can you think of something that can continue to fall but never reach the ground?

A. The temperature

FUN TIME!

Mom: You are such a lazy boy. I cannot believe you got no points on your test.

Son: Actually, the truth is my teacher ran out of stars and so decided to give me the whole Moon instead.

39. **Mercury** has **no moons** and **no atmosphere**, while **Uranus** has at least **27 moons** while **Jupiter** has at least **66 moons.** Uranus was the first planet scientists discovered with a telescope.

40. A **solar eclipse** can only last a total of 7 ½ minutes. The highest number of solar eclipses that can occur within a year on Earth is five.

41. Galaxies have **supermassive black holes** at the center. Even our very own galaxy, the Milky Way, has one. Astronomers can ascertain their existence by studying their effects on gases and stars close to them.

42. It takes Uranus **84 Earth years** to revolve around the sun. It is made up of gases that make it appear blue. Again, Uranus is the only planet that revolves on its side. This means that it has seasons with distinctive characteristics. Winters and Summers at its north and south poles last for 21 years.

43. Planet **Uranus** is full of **Methane** and **Hydrogen**, two highly flammable gases, but why doesn't it burn? That's because oxygen is required for combustion to take place. Uranus lacks enough oxygen for the two flammable gases to burn.

44. Saturn's moon is the second largest in our solar system. This moon is called Titan.

FUN TIME!

There was once a tick on the moon. Can you guess what everyone said it was?

A luna-tic

45. It takes **billions of years** for objects in space to reach the Earth. This means that you may spot something that is no longer in existence, but you can only see the light traveling huge distances before it is visible.

46. Clouds may have an airy and weightless appearance, but they are cumbersome. Scientists report that clouds weigh approximately **1.1 million pounds** on average. That's the weight of 100 elephants combined.

47. How are they able to float? Well, this weight is spread out into millions, if not billions of **droplets** over an extensive space. Some of the droplets are so microscopic, and you would need at least one million of them to make just one raindrop.

47. The moon has **moonquakes**, just like the Earthquakes experienced on Earth. However, the moonquakes are less intense and less common compared to those that happen on Earth.

48. It rains **diamonds** in **Jupiter**. This is because the intense heat and high pressure in the atmosphere of Jupiter and Saturn can squeeze carbon in the clouds and make it fall in the form of diamonds.

49. We can say that **Pluto** isn't even one year old yet, technically. Scientists discovered Pluto in 1930. Being the farthest dwarf planet, it has to travel long distances before completing its path around the sun. Pluto takes **248** Earth years to complete one rotation around the sun. So if we add 278 years to the first time it was discovered (1930+278 years), Pluto's first birthday would be in 2178.

Technical Terms

1. **Galactic Year** – the amount of time it takes for the earth to revolve around the galaxy.

2. **Blackhole** – Black holes are super mysterious and totally invisible. The center of a black hole is dense and compact, and the force of gravity becomes so strong that not even light can escape around it. Giant stars explode at the end of their life cycle to leave behind black holes.

3. **Solar Wind** – the powerful magnetic forces on the Sun's surface create strong winds that blow throughout the solar system. Scientists refer to these winds as solar winds, and it is made of charged particles that are in continuous motion out of the Sun in multiple directions.

4. **Light Year** – The distance traveled by light in a single year. That's 5.9 trillion miles.

NASA (National Aeronautical & Space Administration)

1. There is a famous myth about a pen used by NASA to write in space. NASA used millions of dollars to produce the pen. However, astronauts from the Soviet Union simply used a pencil to write, which didn't cost more than a few dollars to make. No one knows how true this myth is.

FUN TIME!

Math Teacher: Billy, I want to see how well you can count. If you had Ten dollars and you ask your father to give you another ten. How much money will you have?

Billy: I would still have ten dollars, Sir.

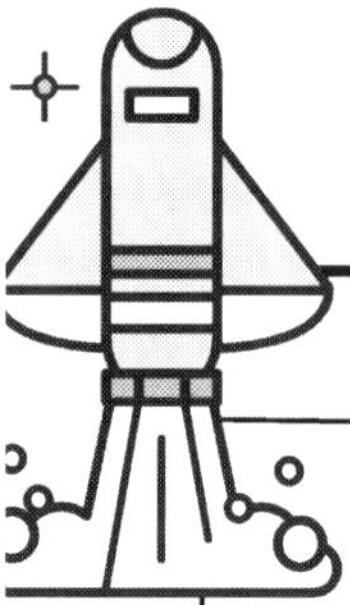

2. An intern called Thad Roberts was arrested and charged with **theft** and contamination of **moon rocks**. He was sent to jail for seven years.

3. It is estimated that a complete **NASA spacesuit** costs a whopping **$12,000,000**. Even more unexpected is the fact that 70% of that cost is for the control module and backpack alone.

4. That was the price of the suit back in 1974. How much would the suit cost today, almost 50 years down the line?

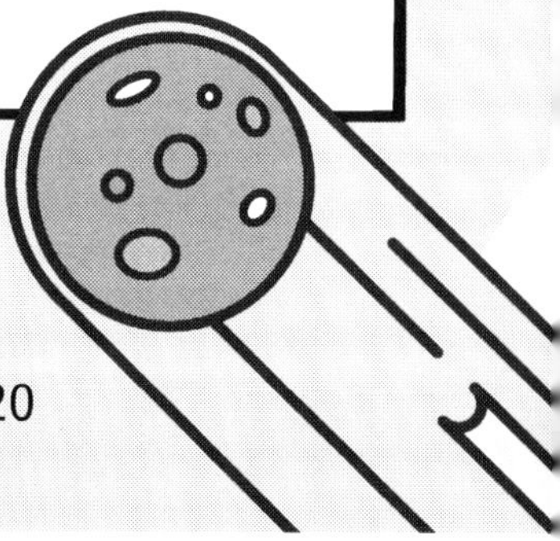

5. If you want to work at **NASA**, you better watch the movie **Armageddon**. Rumors have it that they ask new employees to identify as many scientific inaccuracies as they can after watching the movie.

6. NASA's first project was called **Project Mercury.**

7. Do you love the super **soaker water gun**? Well, a NASA scientist invented it.

8. Tom and Jerry is a cartoon series that has entertained kids for over 80 years. It seems like even NASA scientists were smitten with the characters as much as we were because they named 2 of their satellites **"Tom & Gerry"** and sent them on a mission to orbit around the Earth.

9. The effects of prolonged **weightlessness** are significant in space exploration. NASA pays people to lay in bed for many hours so that they can study this phenomenon.

10. The **International Space Station** has a group of astronauts that have been living and working in space for over **20 years**. The astronauts come from the **United States, Japan, France, and Russia.**

11. Space exploration is so dangerous that the **Apollo astronauts** were unable to qualify for **life insurance**. As a result, insurance companies were cautious about this mission.

12. If the International Space Station passes over **your location,** you will receive a **text message**. How cool! You could show off the text to your friends. They would all be so fascinated

Space Shuttles

1. **Space shuttles** are similar to airplanes and rockets in a few ways. For example, space shuttles land on runways like **airplanes**, they orbit like **spacecraft**, and they take off vertically like **rockets**.

2. NASA has launched five space shuttles; **Atlantis**, **Columbia**, **Challenger**, **Endeavour**, and **Discovery**. Unfortunately, two of them (Columbia and Challenger) crashed, killing 14 astronauts on board.

3. The Space Shuttle system is made up of **four major elements**; an external tank, three very important engines, a pair of solid rocket boosters, and extra add-ons.

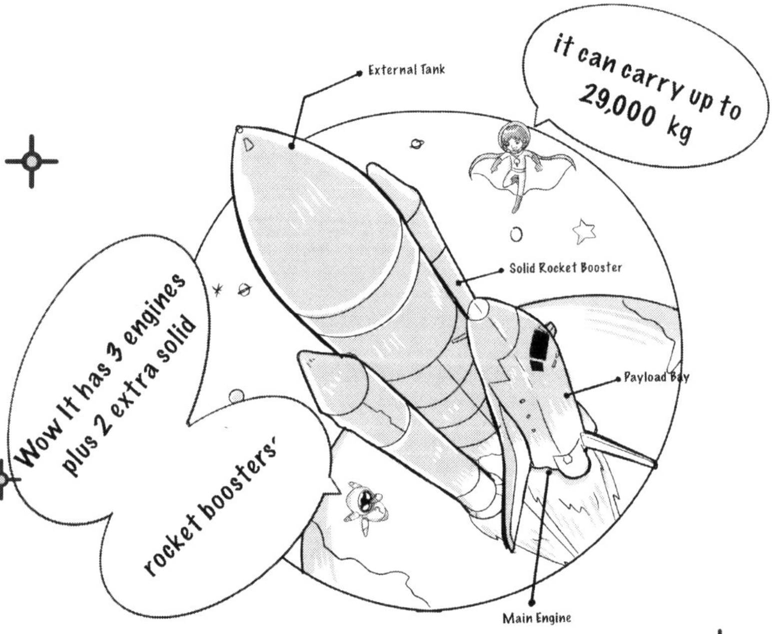

4. The combined distance covered by the five space shuttles is **513.7 million miles.** That is almost double the distance between Earth and Jupiter, which is 365 million miles when they are at their closest point.

5. The **heaviest shuttle** was **Columbia**, with a net weight of 178,000 pounds. Unfortunately, it is one of the two that crashed.

6. **Challenger** shuttle **crashed** and killed the astronauts on board but not before Sally Ride made history as the first American woman in space. It crashed on January 28, 1986.

7. A space shuttle accelerates from **0-17,000 miles per hour** in a matter of **8 minutes** only.

8. The **Columbia** was **destroyed** on re-entry after it had completed 27 missions.

9. The space shuttle has a **liftoff weight** of **4.5 million pounds**.

10. The main engine of the Space shuttle produces as much **horsepower** as **39 train locomotives** combined. In addition, the engine weighs as much as a single train locomotive.

11. Over **600 crew member**s have gone on **shuttle missions**. In addition, over **3 million pounds** of cargo have been sent into space.

12. A Space Shuttle ready to take off is **as tall as** the **Statue of Liberty** but weighs three times as much.

Light

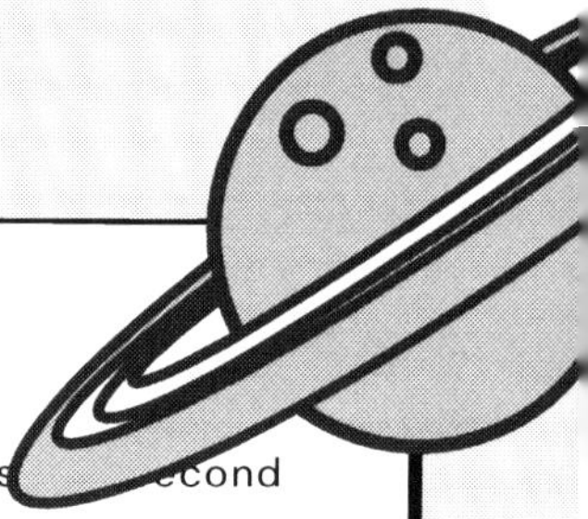

13. **Light** travels at a **speed** of **299,792** kilometers per second on earth (through the air).

14. Light travels faster in **vacuum** (no air) with a speed of **300,000** kilometers per second. That's faster than anything else in the universe.

15. **Animals** see lights differently. For example, dogs can only see objects in **shades of gray**,

16. A red **ladybug** appears red because its body absorbs green and blue light while it **reflects red light**. Our brains instruct us to think that the ladybird is red using some special brain cells.

17. We are only able to see objects because they absorb, reflect, or **give off light**. So, for example, we can see the sun because it gives off its light and we can see the moon because it **reflects light** from the sun.

FUN TIME!

In what situations do people go at red and stop at green?

When they are eating a watermelon.

18. You perceive objects as colored because they reflect only specific wavelengths of light. So, for example, if an object appears red, it reflects all other colors except red.

FUN TIME!

There was an advert in our area that read, "Try the soup that travels at the speed of light."

I thought they should name it "fast food."

19. **Sunlight** is the source of **life**. Without it, all life on the planet would die. Why? Well, plants need sunlight to grow. Likewise, animals and plants require light to process Vitamin D.

20. **Light** is a form of energy made up of microscopic particles called **photons**. It can move in **waves**.

FUN TIME!

What did the photon say to the porter when asked if he needed any help with his bags?

Thank you for the offer, but I am traveling light.

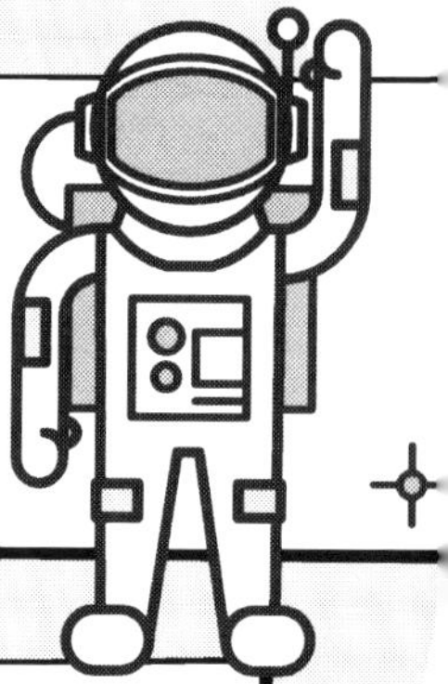

21. Light travels **faster than sound,** and that's exactly why you see a flash of lightning when **thunder** strikes even before you hear it, even though they both happen at the same time.

22. The **light** from the **Sun** appears **white**, but in reality, it is a mixture of the **seven colors** that make up the rainbow. This means that white light can be separated into seven distinct colors (Red, Orange, Yellow, Green, Blue, Indigo, Violet). Furthermore, it can be done using a prism in a process called dispersion.

23. Have you ever wondered how **magnifying glasses** work? They refract light making objects on the **opposite side** appear larger.

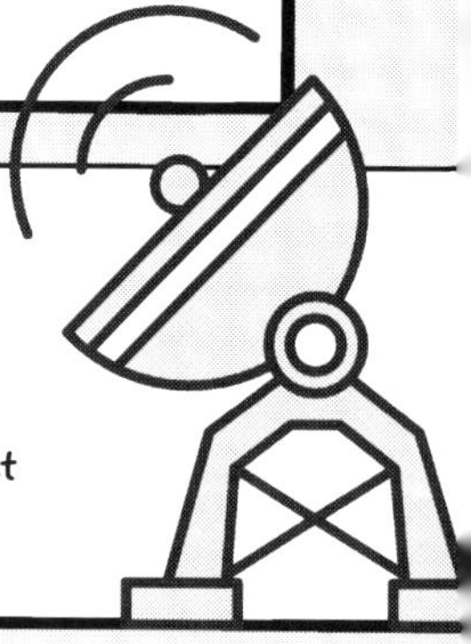

FUN TIME!

Doctor: how much do you weigh?

Patient: With my contact lenses or without my contact lenses?

24. Did you know that astronauts see **stars** during the **day** in space? That's because space has no atmosphere and therefore, it is totally **pitch black**, and the stars can shine through. If Earth had no atmosphere, the sky would be pitch black, and we would have the same experience as astronauts.

25. **Telescopes**, **binoculars**, and **eyeglasses** work by a process called **refraction**. The glass in these objects bends light enough on a focus to the extent where the wearer can actually see the object.

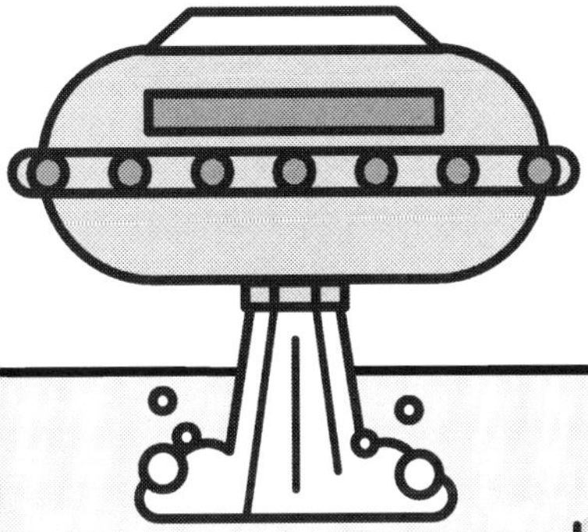

FUN TIME!

I don't usually tell people about my light jokes. I like to keep them in the dark.

CHAPTER 2: BIOLOGY

Biologists are scientists who've dedicated their lives to studying Biology, which is the science of life, how living things behave, their interaction with the environment and their evolution in general. Biologists believe that the earth has more than 10 million different forms of life. This is in addition to the fact that marine biologists have discovered over 1.5 million unique marine creatures and that's not even close to how many they believe are in existence.
For this reason, Biology has been divided into many different branches – Zoology, Botany, Cytology, Anatomy among many others.

Let's explore this fascinating subject.

Human Body

1. The **human body** has a staggering **30 trillion cells** in total. Biologists also estimate the number of bacterias in our body around 40 trillion, most of it in our digestive system.

2. The bone found in your thigh is called the **Femur** and it is the **largest bone** in the human body. It can support up to 30 times your body weight.

Joke Time!

What did the femur say to the patella (kneecap)?
I kneed you.

3. The rhythm of your **heart** is controlled by a complex electric setup called **cardiac conduction**. The heart is very powerful, it weighs approximately one pound, it is made of cardiac muscle and it produces over **100,000 beats** in a single day.

4. Without **saliva**, you would never be able to **taste food**. You are only able to taste the flavor in food when it mixes with saliva.

5. The **cornea** is the only part of your body that has **no blood** supply. This is necessary to ensure that it stays transparent so that you can see clearly. The cornea gets its oxygen supply from the air directly. The human body can also make use of a clear fluid called aqueous humor to transport oxygen instead of the usual red blood cells.

Joke Time!

What did the blood cell say before it died in an artery?
I will not die in vein!

6. If all the **blood vessels** in the human body were to be straightened out, they would circumscribe the Earth four times. Remember that the circumference of the Earth is **24,901 miles**.

7. The **fingernails** on the hand you use for writing **grows faster** than the one you don't use for writing. And what's more, the nails grow faster in longer fingers than in shorter fingers. Also, they grow faster during the day than at night and faster during the summer than during any other seasons.

8. A **runny nose** is annoying, but do you know that's the only way your body flushes out germs from your system when you are down with a cold or flu?

9. The human **brain** has **86 billion nerve cells**. These cells are connected with over **100 trillion bonds**. That's way more than all the stars in the Milky Way combined.

10. Did you know that you can reduce the chances of **tooth decay** by eating **cheese** at the end of a meal? This is because cheese neutralizes the acids in our mouth that can cause tooth decay.

Joke Time!

Why is the longest human nose on record only 11 inches long?

Because if it were 12 inches long, it would be a foot!

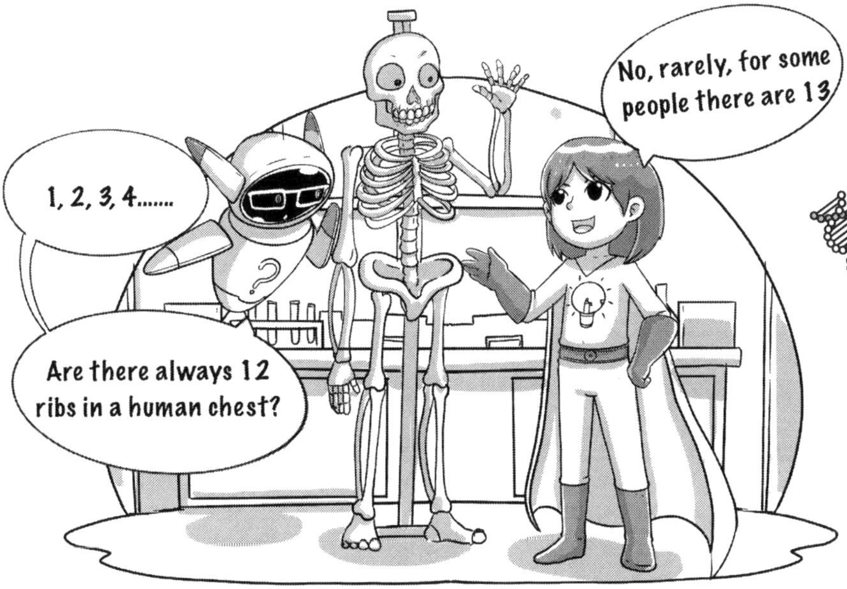

11. Babies only **blink** once or **twice a minute** while adults blink up an average of 10 times a minute. Could this be why babies always appear to be staring?

12. The human **brain** cannot perceive **pain**.

13. The human brain **sends messages** through the human body at 200 miles per hour (**322km/hr**). That's super-fast. If you drove at this speed on the highway, it wouldn't be long until you ran off the road and crashed.

14. The **right side** of your brain **controls** the **left side** of your body, and the left side of your brain controls the right side of your body. So, for example, if you are left-handed, that hand is controlled by your brain's right side.

15. We all know that every person has **unique** fingerprints, but did you know the same theory applies to **tongue prints**? Every person has unique tongue prints.

16. **Women's** hearts beat at a **faster** rate compared to men's hearts.

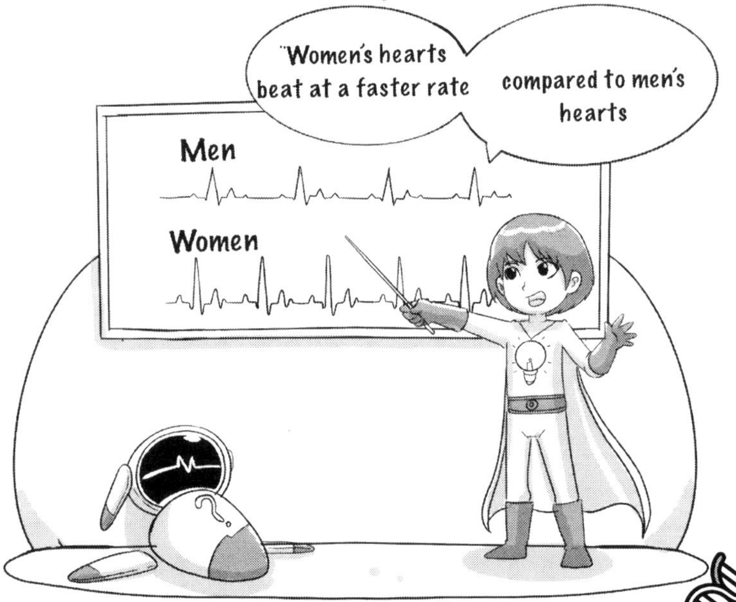

Fun Time!

Where can you see 13 hearts but no other organs?
In a deck of cards.

17. It takes **200 muscles** in the body for an adult to make **one step.**

18. If all the **iron** in **your body** were to be removed, it would be enough to make a **nail three inches long**.

19. Antoine van Leeuwenhoek was the **first person** and biologist tosee a living cell with the help of a **microscope** in 1674.

20. The **human body** produces electricity. But the electric activityis better documented in the brain than in any other part of thebody.

21. The human brain produces at least **0.085 watts** of electricity at any given time. That's enough electricity to light up a bulb or fully charge an iPhone 5C in just under 70 hours.

Fun Time!

What was the sentence of a guilty scientist driving faster than the speed of Light?

Judge: Go to the prism.

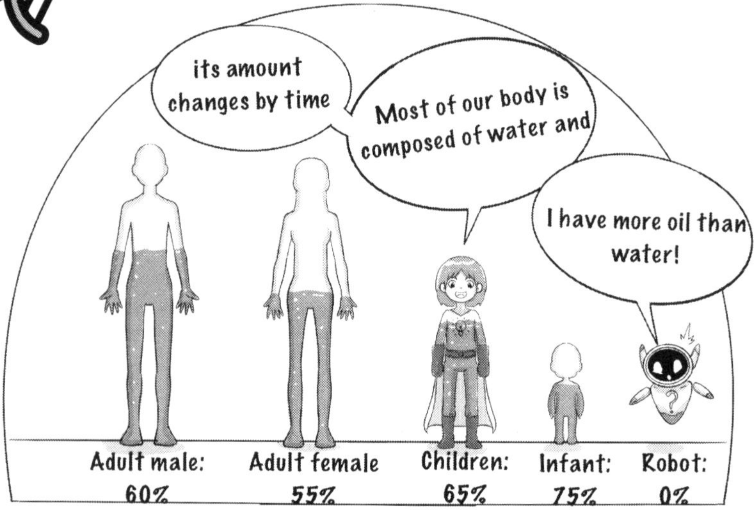

22. The **human body** produces enough **heat** to boil almost two liters (half a gallon)of water.

23. On average, the **brain** of an adult weighs about 3 pounds (1.5kgs) That's approximately 2% of a human's total body weight, yet the brain uses up to 20% of the total energy produced in the body.

24. When you **swallow** your food, it only takes **7 seconds** for it to reach your **stomach**.

25. In reality, the **brain** cannot do **multiple things** at the same time. Even when we are under the impression of **multitasking**, we are not. We are simply switching back and forth from one task to another. It is, therefore, better to focus on a single task at a time, then move on to the next. This way you will improve your efficiency.

26. **Your body** has an average of **four pounds** of **bacteria**. Many of these bacteria are useful. They help with digestion, repair damaged cells and tissues, attack and destroy pathogens, and protect the body against diseases.

27. None of the **computers** that have ever been built are as powerful, clever, or intelligent as the **human brain**. Some experts believe that Artificial Intelligence may surpass the human brainin the near future.

Fun Time!

There is only one occasion when a brain feels fear. When is it?

When the brain loses its nerve.

28. Most people are born with **12 ribs**, but other people have **13 ribs**. This is an extremely rare condition. Can you count your ribs and see if you are one of these special people with an extra rib?

29. Did you know that **babies** have **more bones** than adults? A baby will have a total of 300 bones during birth, but some bones will fuse, and the total number of bones will reduce to 206d uring adulthood.

30. Over **¼ of the oxygen** that enters the human body is used bythe **brain** alone.

31. The small **intestine** in an adult human being is about **18–23 feet**long. That is around four times as tall as an adult human being.S o isn't it a little strange how an intestine this long could fit insuch a tiny space, along with other organs?

32. The jaw is the **strongest muscle** in the human body in ratio to its weight. It is also called the **masseter**. controlled by your brain's right side.

33. When you **blush**, the veins in your face dilate and increase blood supply to your face, making you turn red. But did you know that as this happens, the lining of your **stomach** turns red too?

34. Human beings spend an average of **5 years** of their life **eating**.

35. If your **eye** were used to make a digital camera, it would be a **576-megapixel** camera compared to an iPhone 7 camera with 12 megapixels. So you see, our eyes are exceptional cameras.

36. Your body contains seven **octillion atoms**. An octillion has one followed by 27 zeros (multiply it by 7 to get the total number of bits in a human body). Did you even know such a number exists?

37. Your **nose** can remember up to **50,000 scents**, and your eyes can distinguish 10 million colors.

Fun Time!

Billy, did I see you pick your nose earlier?
No, sir. I have had this nose since the day I was born.

38. The thin membrane under the lungs is called the **diaphragm**. Sometimes it twitches, causing an unexpected intake of air which is then interrupted when the throat closes. This is what we know as **hiccups**.

39. The human **eye** has a total of **2 million working parts**. The part of the eye you see is just around 1/6 of the whole eyeball. The human eye is the second most complex organ in the body after the brain.

40. If all the **skin** in the human body were to be removed and spread out, it would be around **20 square feet**. That's almost the size of a child's blanket. If the skin were to be measured, it would weigh about 4kgs.

Fun Time!

Why are left hands jealous of right hands?
Because they are always right.

41. As small as it may look, the **pinky finger** contributes at least50% of your hand's total strength. Surgeons agree that if youwere to lose the small finger, your hand would lose its ability tograb onto things with a tight grip. If you ever choose to lose afinger, then your best bet would be the index finger.

42. The human **tongue** has around ten **thousand taste buds**, andgirls generally have more than boys. This difference is notexceptional, but it is clear. Women have a refined sense of tastethan men because they recognize sweet and sour flavors better.

43. Every day the **kidney** sends **six cups** (1,500ml)of urine to thebladder. This is because the kidney filters the blood after every45 minutes.

44. Your **brain** is an unbeatable **hard drive**. With over **one billion**nerve cells and over one trillion connections, the brain can store up to 2.5 petabytes of memory. That's as big as leaving yourdigital video recorder running 24 hours a day for three centuries!

45. Throughout his lifetime, an average-sized **man** will consume **33tons of food**. That's like the weight of 6 elephants combined.

46. There is enough **fat** in the human body to make **seven bars** of soap.

47. Did you know that there are around **30 blood group** systems recognized in the medical field? Unfortunately, most of us areonly familiar with the more popular, simplified version known as"ABO," which classifies blood groups as either O, A, B, and AB.

Fun Time!

Why do mosquitoes love blood so much?
There are so many choices of flavors for them to choose from.

48. No other **animals** have **chins** apart from human beings. The jaws of monkeys and chimpanzees are slightly curved inwards, so they don't have chins either.

49. Up to **600,000 particles** of **skin** are shed from the human body every hour. So a large percentage of the dust in your house is these dead cells.

50. **Twenty-one seconds** is the amount of time it takes for an average mammal to empty its **bladder**.

51. If your sense of **smell** were to be blocked, you would never be able to distinguish **potatoes**, **onions**, and **apples**. That's because they all taste the same.

Fun Time!

Why is a person' s nose not on the right or left side of someone's face?

Because it has to be (in) the center.

52. Your **lungs** don't look the same as most people think. Your right lung is divided into **three lobes**, while the left lung is divided into two. The left lung is a little smaller, too, thus creating space for the heart.

53. The surface area of the **lungs** is approximately **70 square meters**. That's approximately ¼ of a tennis court.

54. The human **heart** pumps enough **blood** to fill an Olympic-sized **swimming pool** in a single year.

Fun Time!

Boy: Mum, can I have a cardboard belt like all my friends?
Mum: If you did, then you would have a waist of paper

55. A full-grown adult will **blink** an average of 4.2 million times in a year. Thus, in a single day, a person blinks **12,000 times.**

56. An individual's **personality** can be guessed by observing the shape of their **eyebrows**. People with straight eyebrows are known to be more truthful and direct, while people with slightly curved eyebrows are known to be pleasant, happy, and friendly.

Are you a fact-oriented or people-oriented person according to the shape of your eyebrows?

57. The **nostrils** work **independently**, one at a time. One of our nostrils does most of the breathing at a given time when we breathe in and out during the day. The roles are switched up every few hours. This is precisely why when our nose gets stuffed; it only happens in one nostril.

Fun Time!

What did the skeleton buy at the butcher's shop?

Some spare ribs

Genetics

Why do some people have red hair while others have black hair? Why do other people have blue eyes and others brown?

Well, the science of genetics answers these questions.

Genetics studies the physical and personality traits of a person. It explains why someone looks the way they do, why they have certain talents, and behave a certain way.

Specific characteristics are passed on from parents to their kids. Genes carry these characteristics, and they affect our appearance, personality, and health.

Facts About Genetics

1. If two sets of identical **twins** get married and have kids, their children will be **siblings** according to their genes (their genes have lots of similarities), and they are called **social cousins.**

2. Most of us can see roughly **1 million** different **colors**, but some women have genes that enable them to see up to 100 million different colors.

Fun Time!

What will DNA always wear on a night out?
Jeans

3. There is a certain **gene mutation** that can make the bones **very heavy**. A person suffered from this disease, and his bones were so heavy that he would sink like a stone when he tried to swim. He even came out of a car accident without breakingany of his bones. This person inspired the movie Unbreakable.

Fun Time!

Why does the mother of identical twins, Amal and Juan, only keep a photo of one of them in her purse?

When you've seen Juan, you've seen Amal already.

Animal & Plants

1. Living things are divided into five major kingdoms – **Animals**, **Plants**, **Protists**, **Bacteria**, and **Fungi**. Did you know that viruses have not been classified into any of these kingdoms? Poor guys, it seems like they are uninvited everywhere. Can you guess where they would best fit according to their characteristics?

2. The skin of polar bears is actually black. Their furs are hollow and transparent, meaning they can appear in different colors in different lightings. In reality, polar bears aren't truly white. They appear white because their fur is scattering white sunlight. On a gray, cloudy day, they can appear gray or even reddish-orange during sunset.

Fun Time!

Have you ever seen a bear in a shoe shop?
No, because they always go bear foot.

3. The first mammal to be **cloned** from an adult cell was Dolly, the **sheep**, and she was born on 5th July 1996.

4. Did you know that **earthworms** have **five hearts**? Yet, even then, their circulatory system isn't as complex as that of human beings. That's because the hearts don't need to pump blood to many body parts, as with human beings.

5. Did you know that adult **polar bears** lack **natural enemies**? The only danger to them in their wild habitat is other polar bears.

6. **Rafflesia Arnoldii** is a plant that produces the **largest** individual **flowers** in the world. The flowers can reach a height of 3 feet (1 meter) and a weight of 10kgs.

7. **Female** lions run the **lion kingdom**. They are better hunters than male lions, and they use their expertise to hunt and feed the whole pride. Also, they are good team players and plan to attack their prey.

8. **Elephants** are the **largest** land-based mammals. The most popular species are African bush, African forest, and Asian elephants. They can weigh up to **6300 kg** and grow as tall as 13 feet (4 meters). Elephants need up to **150 kilograms** of **food** per day although half of this may leave the body undigested.

9. Elephants **communicate** in different ways, like trumpet calls, sounds (some are complex for humans to understand or hear), body language, touching or producing scents. They also communicate through **seismic signals** (sounds that create vibrations in the ground), which they may detect through their bones.

10. The **biggest** existing **structure** on this planet is Australia's Great Barrier **Reef**. It is 2000 kilometres (1240) miles long.

11. Do you love **pandas**, **tigers**, and **blue whales**? Unfortunately, these beautiful animals are **endangered species**, meaning they are at risk of being completely wiped out from existence if they are not protected.

Fun Time!

Why are tigers happy that they do not have stripes? Because they never want to be spotted.

12. Did you know that **animals travel to space** frequently? The first living being sent to space was a dog named Laika.

13. It would take a **pineapple** two to **three years** to grow into a full, adult size where it is ready to be consumed. So the chances are that the pineapple you ate recently was grown two years ago.

Fun Time!

Of all the vegetables, why is the mushroom the most popular? Because it' s a fun-gi

14. The only fruits that have their **seeds** on the outside are **strawberries**. They have around 200 seeds.

15. **Wasps** get **drunk**, and that's when they get more aggressive. Have you ever wondered why wasps are more hostile during the **summer**? As soon as they have stored up enough fruit to feed themselves, wasps start to feed on **fermented fruit**, and that's when they start **attacking** other animals aimlessly because they are drunk.

16. You are probably aware that the **platypus** is an egg-laying **mammal**, but do you know that it only lives in **Australia**? It looks like a cross from a **beaver** and **duck** and what's even more mind-blowing is the fact that its offspring cannot suckle from the mammary glands. Instead, they can only suck milk after it pools on her abdomen.

Fun Time!

What do you get when you put three ducks in a box? A box of quakers.

17. Mathias Willemijns grew the **largest pumpkin** in the world. It weighed a whopping **2,624 pounds**. That's close to the average weight of a car. As it is, growing pumpkins as huge as a car is a cool and competitive "sport".

18. You've seen and probably destroyed many **webs**. **Spiders** use very delicate threads to make these webs. The silk may look flexible and light at first glance, but it is actually **stronger** than **steel**. If enough silk were to be harvested and used to make protective gear, they would be strong enough to protect soldiers from **bullets** during combat.

Fun Time!

What did the girl say when some Christmas tree lights got stuck to her head?

Oh my, I feel light-headed.

19. **Cabbage** is very healthy. It has a **91% water** content. Raw **cucumbers** have 96% water, and raw **apples** have 84% water. Apples **float** on water.

20. **Onions** are natural **sedatives**. If you eat too much, they will make you sleepy.

21. The largest **pitcher plant** in the world is known as **Nepenthes rajah**. Being a **carnivorous plant**, the pitcher can capture and eat animals as big as a full-grown rat.

22. Of all trees, **Oaks** are likelier to be struck by **lightning** than any other tree.

Fun Time!

What do trees need to do before they use the internet? They need to log in.

23. There is a species of **grass** found in Africa known as **Elephant grass**. The grass gets its name from its unique characteristics. When it is fully grown, it can be as tall as **4.5 meters** which are high enough for elephants to hide inside if they want to.

24. The **Baobab** tree can store up to **120,000** liters of **water** in its trunk. It is native to Africa.

25. A bunch of **bananas** is called a **hand** and has 10-20 bananas referred to as **fingers**?

26. **Lobsters** have clear **blood**, which turns **blue** when it mixes with oxygen.

27. You will never come across entirely **black flowers**. That's because they don't exist. Currently, we have **very dark** shades of **red** or **purple**.

28. The squid has the **biggest eye** recorded in nature history measuring **10 inches** in diameter.

Fun Time!

What did the leaf say after being pestered by the branch?
Leaf me alone!

CHAPTER 3: HISTORY

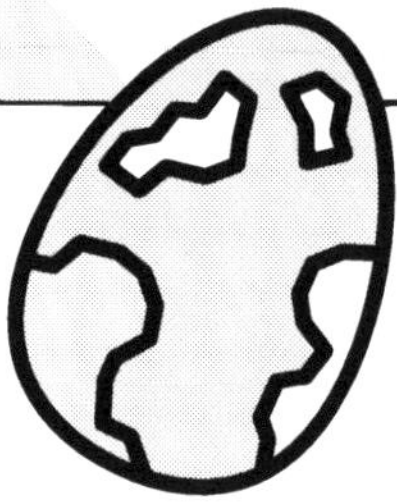

There is an old saying that goes "Those who don't know history are doomed to repeat it". Knowing your history is important and it shouldn't be just about important dates and famous names, but you should also know the details so that you can clearly understand people, their cultures and the eras in which they lived.

Joke Time

What's the history teachers' favorite cake?
Answer: Fruit cake, because it's full of dates

Talk of the most surprising legends and myths or some stories that seem too good to be true, whatever the case, the funniest bits of history are those little facts that are mostly overlooked.

Joke Time

Mum: Billy, come here. How can you explain getting an 'F' in History

Billy: It' s not my fault, mum, everything the teacher talked about happened before I was born.

BUT FIRST...

What’ s B.C. and A.D.?

BC and AD are international standards that were set to count the years based on the traditional setting of the year Jesus Christ was born. A.D. is a Latin abbreviation for the words Anno Domini which refer to the birth of Jesus while B.C. is an abbreviation for Before Christ.

For example, if we say A.D. 2021, it means 2021 after Jes." Some sources use BCE (Before Common Era) and CE (Common Era) for religious neutrality and inclusivity. The abbreviation CE has the same meaning as AD, and BCE the same meaning as BC.

BC. must always appear after the year while AD. Should always come before the year.

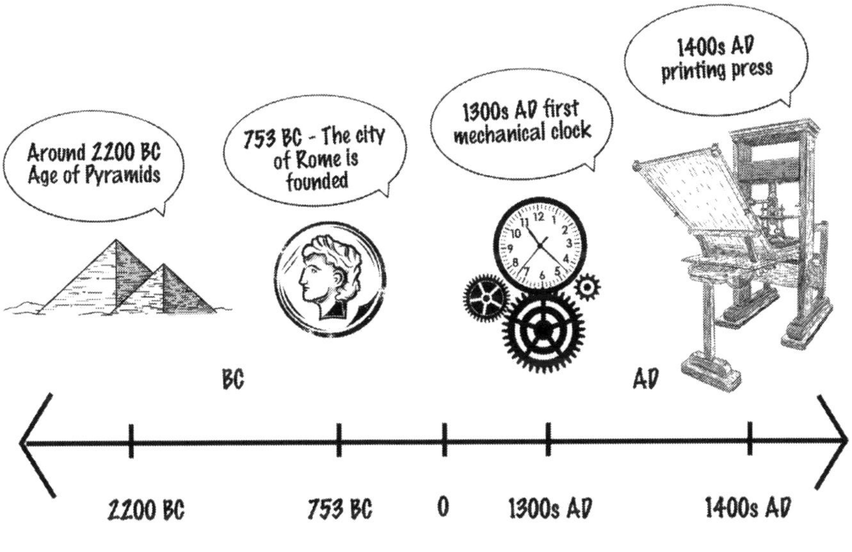

The existence of human beings has been divided into five main ages by historians;

The Prehistoric Era

The prehistoric era is further divided into three short eras based on the technological progress at the time.

a. **Stone Age** – (2.5million B.C to 3000B.C.)

The main highlights of the Stone Age include the use of tools by the earliest humans and Neanderthals and the movement of humans from Africa.

b. **Bronze Age** – (3000B.C. to 1300B.C.)

Refers to the period where the wheel and metalworking were invented. Human beings settled in ancient Egypt, Mesopotamia, and the Indus Valley.

c. **Iron Age** – (1300B.C to 600B.C)

Refers to the period where writing systems, steel, and ironworks were developed. Then, human beings started creating and moving into cities.

Other periods include;

The **Classical Era** (600B.C. to A.D. 476) refers to an eraduring civilizations aroundthe Mediterranean Sea, such as Ancient Rome, Persia, Greece, and Byzantine Empire, prospered.

FUN TIME!

What would you use if you wanted to cut the sea in half? A see-saw, of course!

The **Middle Ages** (A.D476 to A.D.1450). This period is also known as the Dark Ages because a lot of recorded history was lost after the collapse of the Roman Empire.

FUN TIME!

Boy: Dad, our History teacher, said we would talk about the Dark Ages next week. Why would people call them that?

Dad: Because they were full of knights.

Early Modern Era (A.D. 1450 to A.D. 1750). This is the period that follows the Middle Ages directly. It was an era that saw the growth of philosophies and values from famous people such as William Shakespeare, Christopher Columbus, Leonardo Da Vinci, and Johan Sebastian Bach.

Modern Era (A.D. 1750 to present day). This is a period of advanced technological boom and enlightenment. It is also known as the Late Modern Era. The modern era saw an end to the monarchy, war and politics, and revolutions in most countries.

Egypt

Ancient Egypt was a civilization concentrated along the Nile River in North Africa. Its location was in present-day Egypt. It lasted for almost 300 years until it was conquered by Alexander the Great (from around 3100B.C. to 332 B.C).

The great pyramids of Egypt and how powerful the kingdom was is something that historians have always been interested in.

FUN TIME!

What did one pyramid say to the other?
How' s your mummy!

The study of ancient Egypt has grown into a vibrant field of study known as Egyptology.

Here are some facts about ancient Egypt;

1. Make-up was worn by both men and women in ancient Egypt. Green eye paint was made from copper, and Lead was used to make black eye make-up. Egyptians believed that make-up had powerful healing powers, and it protected them from harmful sun rays too.

FUN TIME!

Q. What did the Egyptian put on her face before she went to a Halloween party?
A. Some mas-scare-a

2. Cleopatra was a very powerful Egyptian ruler. She is still as famous today as back then, but did you know that she wasn't actually Egyptian? As a descendant of general Ptolemy, from Macedonia, she was actually Greek but born in Egypt.

3. Cats were worshiped in Egypt as if they were gods. People believed that owning a cat in the house would bring luck upon the household. Modern-day cats are still bossy, though. So could it be that theystill think they're gods and should be treated as such?

FUN TIME!

What's Egyptian comic book language?
Hero-glyphics

4. Do you love playing board games with your friends? Well, so did the Egyptians. One of the most popular board games played by ancient Egyptians was called Senet. They threw sticks instead of dice to calculate how many steps forward someone was supposed to move.

5. Most Egyptian pharaohs (Egyptian rulers) were overweight, unhealthy, and suffered from lifestyle diseases such as diabetes. In addition, the Egyptian diet mainly consisted of wine, honey, bread, and beer, which made many royals overweight even though much of their art depicts them as slim, healthy figures.

6. Did you know that ancient Egyptians were great inventors? They invented keys and locks, papers, pens, and even toothpaste. Egyptians were very skilled.

7. The largest Egyptian pyramid is called the Pyramid of Khufu, and it is found in Giza. This mind-blowing pyramidweighs as much as 16 Empire State buildings combined. Itwas built 4600 years ago. Some experts believe that ron had not been invented at this time.

FUN TIME!

One night, while King Tutankhaum was sleeping, he had a bad dream. Can you guess what he said?

I want my mummy

8. The youngest pharaoh who ruled ancient Egypt was a nine-year-old boy known as Tutankhamun.

9. More than 130 pyramids, most of which were built for pharaohs and their families, have been discovered in Egypt to date. Egyptian pyramids are the oldest stone structures in the world. While Egypt may be famously known for its pyramids, it may be interesting to know that there are more pyramids in South America than Egypt.

10. Stone slabs were used as pillows in ancient Egypt. It seems a little uncomfortable, right?

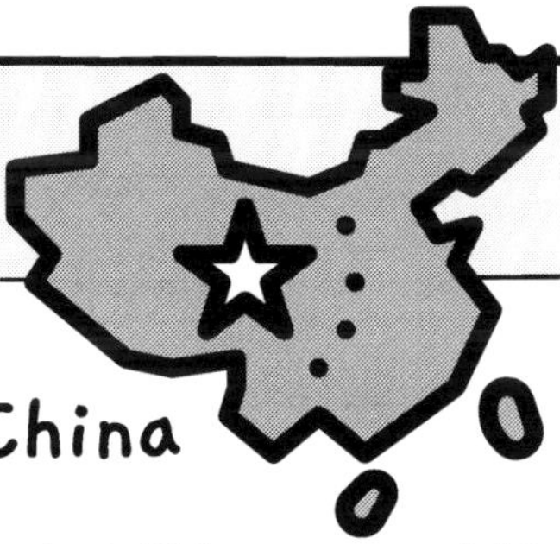

China

Ancient China was a mighty empire, but it is known as the longest civilization in history. The territory was located in the Eastern part of Asia. The history of this empire can be traced to 4,000 years back. Its era lasted from 1600-221 BC.

Here are some fun facts about ancient China:

1. The most successful pirate in the world was a lady. Shewas called Ching Shih. She was part of a fleet known asRed Flag Fleet, where she served as an active commander for her husband.

2. China celebrates its New Year for 15 days. That's more than two weeks, and it sounds like they have a lot of fun. Would you not like to go there and participate in this eventful ceremony?

3. Soldiers in ancient China wore paper armor to protect themselves during battle. As a result, they were the first people to invent paper, gunpowder, and saddle. But protective gear made of paper doesn't seem very helpful, does it?

4. Did you know that brides in China wear red gowns? This is because the Chinese people believe that the color red brings good luck.

FUN TIME!

Can you see that Chinese guy with a camera around his neck? His name is Phil Ming.

5. All pandas on Earth are from China. So if you come across a panda in your country, know that China probably lent it to your country. Even more fascinating is the fact that pandas eat all day long. Up to 16 hours of their days are spent eating. So, do you think they are overweight?

6. The earliest **chopsticks** were invented 5,000 years ago in China. The Chinese used them for cooking and not eating like we do today. So, if anything, chopsticks are the oldest tools of eating that have stayed the same throughout the centuries, not more than bare hands, of course.

7. China's **economy** is the **second-largest** in the World after the United States of America.

8. Did you know that **Hong Kong**, a very big city in China. It has the highest number of **skyscrapers** in the world? It has more skyscrapers than either Dubai or New York.

9. You better thank our good Chinese friends if you are an **ice cream** lover. They invented ice cream **4,000** years ago. This sweet dessert was created using snow, rice mixture, and milk back in the day. This original ice cream had less sugar and was therefore healthier.

10. China has the highest population in the world. According to a report published by the United Nations, the country had a population of 1.4 billion people as of September 2020.

11. Living together as a big family is a sign of wealth in China. As a result, the elderly are highly respected, and laws have been created to protect all aging family members.

12. The largest man-made structure in the world is found inChina. It is called the **Great Wall of China,** and itstretches as far as 8,850 kilometres (**5,500 miles**). Thisstructure is also the largest **graveyard** in the world. Manyworkers died in the building process, and they were thenput in the walls. The stones in this wall were boundusing mortar made of **sticky rice**. Who would have thought rice could be this powerful?

FUN TIME!

Mum: Where can I go see something that is purple and over 5000 miles long?

Son: I do not know
Mum: the grape wall of China.

13. On average, a skyscraper is built in China every **five days**. Thus, at least 73 skyscrapers are built in China every year.

14. If all the railways in China were tied together, they wouldgo around the Earth twice. The Chinese also have one of the fastest train systems in the world.

15. Ketchup is very popular in the US, but did you know that it originates from China? The word ketchup was invented fromthe Chinese word “ke-tsiap” a Chinese sauce made from fermented fish.

16. Most emperors in ancient China believed that they were descendants of dragons.

FUN TIME!

Q. Why did the dragon go to bed at noon and set its alarm for 8:00 pm?
A. It wanted to fight knights.

12. Tang of Shang was a 7th-century Chinese emperor who had 94 special laborers called icemen. The icemen made ice cream. I wonder what his favorite flavors were.

13. How can it be that China, being as big as the USA, has only one official time zone when America has four official time zones? Ask your history teacher this question the next time you see them.

FUN TIME!

I heard Mark Zuckerberg visited Beijing because he wanted to visit the, "Great Firewall."

Rome

Ancient Rome started as a small town located on the Tiber River in central Italy. Ancient Rome ruled Britain, western Asia, the Mediterranean Islands, northern Africa, and continental Europe at its peak.

Rome was founded by twin brothers Remus and Romulus in 753B.C. It was later dissolved in 476 A.D.

FUN TIME!

Q. What is the last thing monkeys take off before they go in the shower?
A. Their Chimpantsies

1. Did you know that monkeys were one of the most popular pets in the Roman Empire? Monkeys were used for entertainment. They must have been cute and funny, right?

2. Caligula was a Roman Emperor who loved his horse so much that he made it a senator. The horse lived like a king. It was given an ivory manger, a collar with precious jewels, a marble stall, and a house.

3. Romans, just like the Egyptians and Persians, were smart inventors. For example, Romans invented the central heating system, calendars, concrete, newspapers, and books.

4. The Colosseum in Rome is the largest ancient amphitheatre ever built in world history up to this day.

5. Romans were exciting people. They ate dinner lying down on couches, and some of their favorite dishes included strange food like flamingos, parrots, and peacocks.

6. Romans loved proper hygiene, but they didn't use soap while bathing. They used oil instead, and then they would scrape off the oil using special scrapers.

FUN TIME!

A Roman man went to the doctor with a cold. What did he say when the receptionist asked him for his name?

Julius Sneezer

7. Crazy as it may sound, ancient Romans washed theirclothes in urine. This is because urine contains ableaching agent called ammonia, which is why Romans collected it to do their laundry.

8. Purple clothing was a symbol of social status in ancientRome. Only senators and emperors were allowed to wear utterly purple outfits. a "normal" person wearing purple was illegal.

9. Some roads built by ancient Romans are still in use today. 55 00 miles of roads built by the Romans are still standing in the UK.

10. Rome wasn't always the capital city of Italy as we know it today. Florence was the capital city of Italy until 1870, when Rome was awarded the title.

11. The first shopping mall was built in Rome by an Emperor called Trajan. The mall was named after the ruler – Trajan's Market.

12. The Statue of Liberty is a famous monument in the USA. Itis a symbol of freedom for all human beings. Well, thisfamous statue was inspired by the Roman goddess known as Libertas.

FUN TIME!

Mum: Andy, why did you get detention today?

Andy: Because in my History test, question one was 'Where was the Declaration of Independence signed," and I wrote, "at the bottom".

13. Our modern day calendar is actually more than 2,000 years old. A Roman ruler called Julius Caesar invented it according to his understanding of the Earth's movement around the sun. Even the months of the year are named after Roman gods. Julius Caesar named July after himself.

14. Present-day Paris was once a Roman city known as Lutetia.

15. Italy has many fountains. One of the most famous fountains is the Trevi Fountain. Legends have it that it will come true if you throw a coin in a rush and make a wish. So every night, 3,000 coins are collected from the fountain and then donated to charity.

FUN TIME!

What has a head and a tail but cannot be killed?
A coin

16. Cats are free animals in Rome. They can roam the city as much as they like, and no one is allowed to chase them away. Cats are protected by the law, which permits them to live freely wherever they are born. If you visit Rome today, you will come across hundreds of cats just walking and resting among people.

17. The war between Romans and Persians could have been the longest in history. It went on for 721 years. The war was passed one from one generation to another for almost one millennium.

FUN TIME!

What did the soldiers use to cut Rome into two?
They used a pair of Caesars.

Persia

Persia was founded by Cyrus the Great, and it was located in Western Asia, present-day Iran. It was the largest empire in the world by the 5th century B.C. It was founded in 550 BC and was later dissolved in 330 BC.

Here are some fun facts about Persia

1. We already know that Egyptians were smart inventors, but could Persians be better than them? Persians invented the first air conditioners and refrigerators. The first Persian refrigeration system was known as yakhchal, and it was made of clay. At first, they used it to store ice, but eventually, it was used to store and keep food fresh for longer.

FUN TIME!

My mother has just given me a new game for my birthday. It' s cool. What you have to do is paint pictures of Ancient Iran.

The game is called the Prints of Persia.

2. Persians celebrate birthdays, serving special foods followed by a cake with candles on it, just like we do today. The concept of celebrating a birthday started as a festival to mark the day a king was born, but all Persians quickly adopted the practice.

FUN TIME!

Willie: Rob, what did you do when that Persian guy wanted to fight you?
Rob: I-ran.

3. Did you know that Persia is present-day Iran? The name Iran was adopted from the word "Aryans," among the first tribes to settle in the region. The name was officially changed to Iran in 1935.

4. Persians developed one of the earliest and most advanced postal systems. Darius I, a Persian ruler, ordered road networks to be built to improve transport. The improved transport system included a messenger service where riders could carry messages back and forth between various capitals.

The art and science of hiding messages inside other messages are known as Steganography. Persians were the first people to use it. They would tattoo messages on their messengers' heads and let the hair grow back (which would perfectly hide the messages) while traveling to their destination.

5. Persians are very truthful people. Telling lies is considered a very disgraceful thing to do.

FUN TIME!

My Persian friend is the funniest guy I know. His jokes are so Iran-ic.

Mayans and Aztecs

Mayans and Aztecs lived in present-day Mexico. The Maya people occupied southern Mexico and some parts of northern Central America from 2600 BC. The Aztecs occupied central Mexico from the 14th-16th century.

FUN TIME!

Woman 1: My indigenous neighbor is a wonderful man. He is so polite and respectful. He also treats his wife well.

Woman 2: Wow. he sounds like a real gentle mayan.

Here are some fun facts about Mayans and Aztecs :

1. The Aztecs were a powerful empire that ruled Mexico for around 300 years. But, did you know that they discovered chocolate? They made and enjoyed a drink that is very similar to modern-day hot chocolate.

FUN TIME!

Which piece of candy never arrives on time?
ChocoLATE of course

FUN TIME!

Boy 1: I have just invented something new. It is a kitten that I have dipped in melted chocolate.

Boy 2: That sounds great. What are you going to call it?
Boy 1: A kitty kat bar

2. Just like the Egyptians, the Aztecs also built pyramids and temples for their rulers and emperors. Their cities were huge and vastly populated. They built canals as well.

3. The Aztecs valued maize (corn) so much that one of their gods was named after it. The god was called Centeotl, which means "Maize cob Lord" when translated. It was their primary diet – just like wheat is a staple to Europe and rice in Asia.

4. Chocolate was so important to the Aztecs that they even used cacao beans as a form of currency. The cacao beans were used to make small purchases, but the cotton cloth was used to make larger purchases.

FUN TIME!

If Aztecs made a ham and cheese sandwich, what would they fill the bread with?

Mayan-naise

5. Aztec had one of the largest capital cities in the world -- Tenochtitlan. With a population of about 300,000 people, Tenochtitlan was as big as five London cities combined.

6. The Aztecs believed that dogs were a guide to heaven. A dead person would be buried with a dog so that it could guide them into the afterlife.

7. The Aztecs first saw horses during the Spanish invasion of their empire. They were so surprised by these beings. Because they had never seen horses, the Aztecs could not help but think that the horse and the riders were one, which greatly affected them mentally.

8. Do you love the color blue? Well, so did the Mayans. Many of their stones, monuments, and walls were painted blue. Blue was also associated with Chaak, the Mayan rain god.

9. Mayans were the first people to domesticate turkeys. Turkeys were very important in Mayan culture. They were even worshipped as gods. Their meat was used for meat, while the bones and feathers would make toys, tools, instruments, and fans.

FUN TIME!

Q: If a big turkey is a gobbler, what is the baby turkey?
A: Call it Goblet

10. Did you know that schooling was compulsory in the Aztec empire, both at school and at home? The schools were divided by gender and social class.

11. Did you know that Mayans **invented** the concept of **zero**? Mayans lived in present-day Mexico and other places in Central and South America. They were well ahead of their years, and they even invented zeros during their math calculation. Their calendars were also very accurate. Experts believe that the calendar correction was 10,000th of a day, more accurate than the modern one used today. Calendars used by Mayans and Mesoamericans are believed to be the most complicated and detailed.

2.

Vikings

Vikings were a native warrior tribe occupying the Scandinavian regions of Sweden, Norway, and Denmark. They were powerful and vicious fighters, and they conducted many successful raids in western and eastern Europe.

Here are some fun facts about Vikings:

1. Popular words in the English dictionary have their origin in the Viking language, which is famously known as the Old Norse language. Such terms include anger, snort, lamp, etc.

FUN TIME!

How did the Vikings secretly communicate with each other?
By norse code

2. Did you know that Viking gods are the inspiration behind the names of day the week? Can you guess which days of the week are named after Viking gods Tyr, Frigg, Woden, and the most famous Thor? You should have Tuesday, Friday, Wednesday, and Thursday if you guess all of them right.

3. Vikings never wore helmets and especially not the ones with horns, as most people believe. Christians invented the idea of them wearing horned helmets in Europe to make the Vikings look even scarier.

FUN TIME!

Where do Viking babies sleep?
In a norsery

4. It may sound a little odd, but most Viking men weren't always fighting enemies and rowing boats. Instead, many of them were farmers who cultivated oats, barley, and rye throughout the year—they domesticated farm animals such as sheep, goats, pigs, and cattle. And the farmers made very good soldiers also.

5. Isn't it interesting that Vikings never referred to themselves as Vikings? Vikings is a term that was invented in the 19th century. Other people and nations called them Danes, Norse, or Norsemen.

FUN TIME!

What are little Viking children' s favorite songs?
Norsery Rhymes

6. Being blonde was every Viking's desire. Blondes were considered beautiful, and even brunette men used extreme tactics to lighten their hair so that they could feel more desirable.

7. Vikings had excellent hygiene and were well-groomed. As a result, some of the most commonly used Viking tools uncovered by scientists are those used for grooming. They include razors, tweezers, and combs which were made from bones and antlers of wild animals.

8. Skiing was a beloved hobby among Vikings. This hobby was a popular recreational sport, and many Vikings saw it as a reliable form of movement. They even worshiped Ullr, a skiing god.

FUN TIME!

I have a Viking friend who does not eat meat or anything else from animals. He calls himself a Norvegan.

9. The only sweet than most Vikings were familiar with washoney. Honey was also used to make many things, including a strong alcoholic drink called mead.

10. Swords were their most valuable possession. Not only were they expensive, but they were also crafted expertly. Unfortunately, most Vikings couldn't afford a sword.

World Wars

The First World War (WWI) started on 28th July 1914 and ended on 11th November 1918. The Second World War (WWII) began in 1939 and ended in 1945. World War II was more of a continuation of World War I: more like a settlement of old scores.

World War II was the most significant conflict in history.

1. Did you know that Russia suffered the highest number of deaths in World War II? Over 21 million Russians lost their lives in the war.

   World War II had a massive impact on the world. The American defense budget grew from $1.9 billion to a whopping $59.8 billion between 1940-1945.

FUN TIME!

My cousin said he found the army confusing. His corporal told him he had joined the army to die, but he said, 'no Sir, I joined the army yester-die'

3. Did you know that 80% of Soviet (present-day Russia) males born in 1923 perished in World War II?

4. Did you know that the Battle of the Atlantic was the longest battle of World War II? It went on for six years, from 1939-1945.

FUN TIME!

Why did the student do her math homework on the floor?
Because her teacher told her to do her work without tables.

5. Seven million rifles and 3 million machine guns were built in America during World War II. As if that wasn't enough, 89,000 tanks, 650,000 jeeps, and 300,000 military aircraft were made during the same period.

6. It may sound strange, but Adolf Hitler's nephew served in the US Army during World War II. He was called William Hitler, a name which he quickly changed after the war.

FUN TIME!

I' m sick of all these World War II jokes on here!
Anne Frankly, they are terrible!

7. Henry Ford founded the Ford Motor Company. On hisdesk, Hitler kept a picture of the Ford founder. Meanwhile,Henry Ford also had a picture of Adolf Hitler on his desk inMichigan, USA. Why you may wonder why they had eachother's photos, we may never know.

8. The camouflage print designs worn by American militarymen in World War II were designed by Norvell Gillespie, aBetter Homes and Gardens editor.

9. Did you know that a 12-year-old boy known as Calvin Graham enlisted in the US army? He had already earned a Purple Heart, and a Bronze Star by the time the Navy found out his age. He must have been a courageous boy.

10. World War II has gone down in history books as the most destructive war of all time. Not only did it cost alotofmoney, but it also killed more people and damaged moreproperty than any other war.

CHAPTER 4: SCIENCE

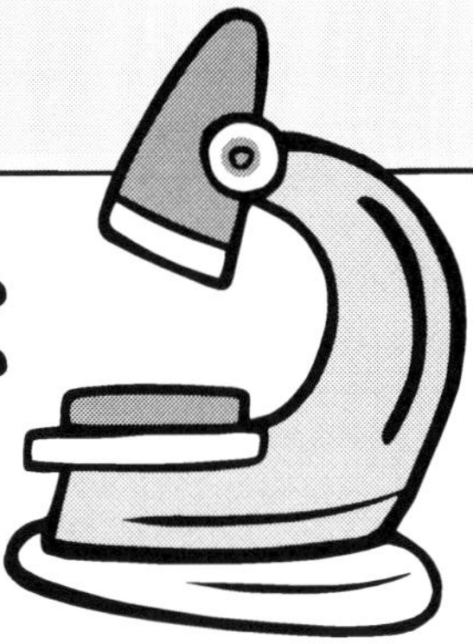

Chemistry and Physics

Chemistry is a branch of science that analyzes the chemical composition, structure, properties, and chemical transformation of different elements. Experts who specialize in this branch of science are called chemists. Chemistry is interesting.

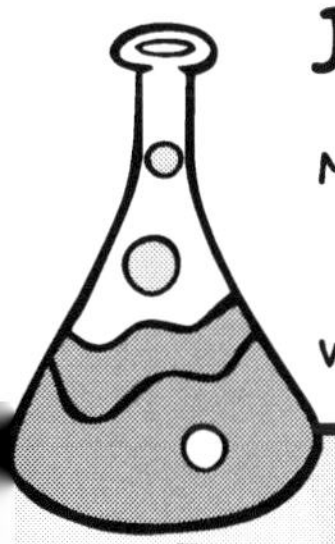

Joke Time

My wife is a chemist, and she is always saying how much she likes "nitrates".

When I ask why she says they are cheaper than "day rates".

Physics is the study of matter and energy and how they behave. Scientists trained in this field are called physicists.

Some of the facts mentioned below will leave you with more questions about the world, some will intrigue you, and others will surprise you.

1. **Mercury** and **bromine** are the only **solid** elements that take on a **liquid** state at **room temperature**. However, the element gallium can also melt quickly. The warmth of your hand is enough to change it from a solid to a liquid state.

2. Did you know that **water expands** when **frozen**, unlike most elements? When water is frozen, it will take up to 9% more space than liquid form. That's why sometimes metal pipes crack during the winter because the water expands while the metal shrinks.

Joke Time

I once asked my chemist wife how she was so good at solving problems. She said it was because she had so many solutions.

3. **Hot water** can **freeze** much **faster** than cold water. Even most scientists find this phenomenon quite surprising. Ancient scientists such as Aristotle and Descartes had described this phenomenon many centuries ago. Still, it was reintroduced into the modern science community by a high school boy from Tanzania known as Mpemba.

4. For this reason, this phenomenon is known as the Mpemba effect. So, next time you observe something interesting, remember to do more research about it. You may discover something new and end up with your name in history.

5. Did you know that the **Moon** has **lesser gravity** compared to the Earth? A man who weighs **70 kgs** on Earth would weigh **11.5 kgs** on the moon. That is quite a huge difference. Can you add up how much you would weigh on the moon?

6. Do you know the **chemical name for water** (H_2O)? Can you guess from the chemical combination? It is dihydrogen monoxide, which basically means two hydrogen molecules and one oxygen molecule.

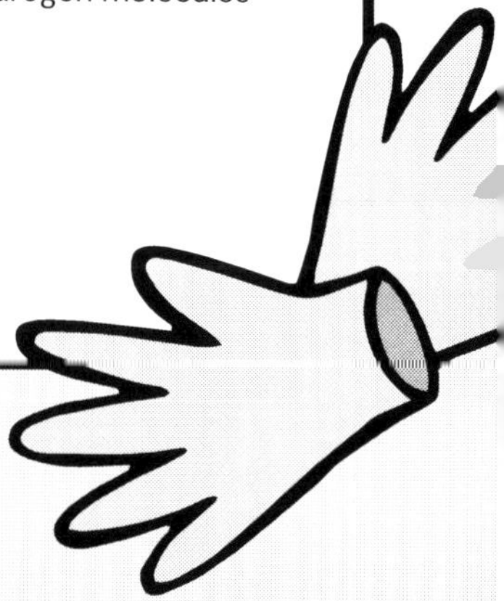

Joke Time

Mum: Alice, how did you do on your Chemistry test.
Alice: I only got one question wrong. It was about the chemical formula for water. I wrote H-I-J-K-L-M-O.

Mum: Really! Why did you think that was the answer?
Alice: Because in class last week the teacher said it was H to O

6. Did you know that **mosquitoes** are more likely to bite **women** than men? That's because females emit more heat from their bodies, and the heat attracts insects. Mosquitoes detect their prey based on their heat and sweat emissions.

7. Did you know that the **sting** of a **wasp** is **alkali** while that of a **bee** is **acidic**? So, is a bee sting the remedy for a wasp sting and vice versa? I mean, the two chemicals are opposites, and they can neutralize each other.

Fun Time

Why did the bee get angry at the hair salon?

Because the hairstylist used a "honey-comb," and it made the bee's hair sticky.

8. **Electric fields** and **gravity** work pretty much the **same** way. The only difference is that electric fields can either attract or repel objects, while gravity can only attract things to themselves.

9. **Glenn Seaborg** is a scientist famously known for being the only person who could write his **address** in the form of **chemical elements**. Can you write your address using elements from the periodic table?

Fun Time

What do you call an indecisive bee?
A may-be

10. You will have lost at least **1% of the water** in your body by the time you feel **thirsty**. So drink water regularly, don't wait until you are thirsty.

11. Did you know that **cooking** is **chemistry**? Yes, that's right. The heating process of cooking brings chemical changes in the food, making it edible. For example, as you eat meat, the protein starts to denature, the color changes, the meat loses its water and becomes dry as you continue cooking it.

Fun Time

What would an Arab leader order to drink in a health food restaurant?
A protein Sheikh

In reality, **glass is actually liquid.** The glass molecules still flow, but the movement is so slow that the human eye can barely see it. This slow movement of glass molecules is not enough to classify it as a liquid, nor is it realistic to say it is solid. Scientists, therefore, classify glass as an amorphous solid – a state that is neither liquid nor solid.

12. The gaseous state of **oxygen** is colorless, but the **solid** and **liquid** forms of **oxygen are blue**.

13. Dare your friend to find the **letter J** on the **periodic** table and watch them slowly realize that it is the only letter that doesn't appear on the periodic table.

Fun Time

In which city are you most likely to get hurt?
Electri-city

14.. Did you know that **energy** can be transformed into **many forms**? For example, when lightning occurs, the energy is transformed into **sound**, **heat**, and **light**.

15. **13%** of the world's **electricity** is produced by **nuclear** energy.

16. They may be small, but **ants** have certain **superpowers** that humans don't have. For example, humans can't see the **ultraviolet** light region, but ants can see it clearly.

17. **One inch** of **rain** can create **10 inches of snow** when the temperature is 0 degrees Celsius.

18. If you pour a handful of **salt** into a **glass of water**, the volume of the water will reduce by up to **2%**. That's because the salt molecules become more organized and packed in the presence of the water molecules.

19. The **Dead Sea** is a true wonder of physics. The **high salt** levels in the water make it so **dense** that a person can easily **float** on the water. So we can all enjoy the Dead Sea even if we are not excellent swimmers.

Fun Time

Ghost 1: Where do you want to go on holiday?
Ghost 2: I don' t know. Somewhere I can swim every day, I guess.
Ghost 1: I know. We can go to the Dead Sea.

20. **Black holes** aren't black, as you might think. Stephen Hawking, a famous physicist, discovered that the black hole has radiation that makes it glow in a way that it gives off light across a broad graphite spectrum.

21. **Diamonds** and **graphite** are made of the **exact compound - carbon**. Diamonds are beautiful, very rare, and quite honestly expensive. It is a crown jewel. Graphite, on the other hand, is nothing more than a pencil leads to most of us.

Fun Time

Jack: Do not listen to Mary' s jokes. They are like a (blunt) pencil.
Brenda: What do you mean?
Jack: They have no point.

22. Only the **arrangement of carbon** inside diamond and graphite is different, which makes them unique.

23. The largest **hydroelectric power station** in the world is found in **China**. It is called The Three Gorges Dam.

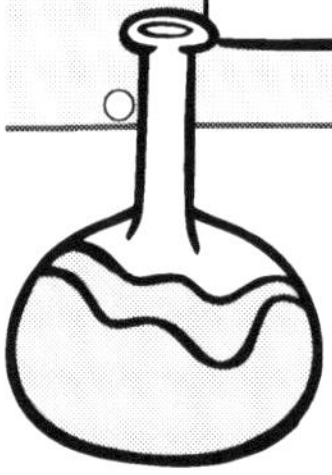

Fun Time

What greeting does the beach give to the sea every time it comes in?
Hello! Long time, no sea.

24. **Astatine** is the rarest **naturally occurring element** on the surface of the Earth. Therefore, if a scientist needs it, then they have to create it from scratch. Even then, only 0.00000005 grams of this element has been successfully made.

25. No other liquid dissolves more materials than water.

Fun Time

Do you know what is the matter with the world?
I do. It' s solid, liquid, and gas.

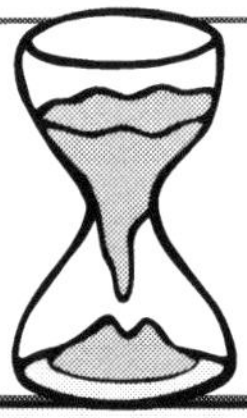

26. **DNA** is **not susceptible** to **fire**. It cannot catch on fire. The chemical structure of DNA has a combination of elements such as **ammonia** and **phosphate**, which do not support burning. Scientists hope to create inflammable clothing in the near future by coating fabric with DNA.

27. The average **adult body** has approximately **0.4 pounds** of salt (**NaCl**).

28. Most **molecules** are **microscopic**. We can barely see them with our naked eyes. This isn't the case with rubber tires – they are a single, giant-sized molecule. In simple terms, tires are made up of large polymers held together by strong covalent bonds.

29. Your **body** is **actually water**. **70%** of the human body is composed of water. But what's even more interesting is that this volume of water **keeps on changing** at different stages of our lives.

30. For the **first few months** of its life, a human fetus consists of **95% water**; at birth, the water reduces to around **77%**, in **adults**, the water reduces even further to about 60-70%. Thus, a 70kg person has around 42 liters in their body.

31. Did you know that your **bones** contain **31% water?** The **skin** has **64% water**. The kidneys and muscles contain 79% water, and **70%** of the **human brain** is also made of water. Our cells contain more than 2/3 of all the water in our entire body.

Fun Time

Can I mention something that is guaranteed to make your face smile? It' s your face muscles.

32. The state of **Hawaii** has the world's **most beautiful rainbows**. When it rains, the mountains produce sharp gradients, which produce beautiful rainbows for people to see.

33. The **largest solar power** plant is found in the **USA**. It is located in the **Mojave Desert**.

34. **Coal** is the **largest producer** of energy used to generate **electricity** in the world. The coal is used to heat water and turn it into steam which is then used to spin turbines connected to generators that produce the electricity.

35. **Astronauts** become **slightly younge**r because of **relativity**. That's because the speed of time is affected by both **gravity and velocity.** Space has no gravity nor velocity. Because of these two factors, time travels very slowly in space.

Fun Time

Ellie: I have an astronaut friend who stood on some chewing gum last week?

Penny. What happened to him?
Ellie: The poor man got stuck in Orbit.

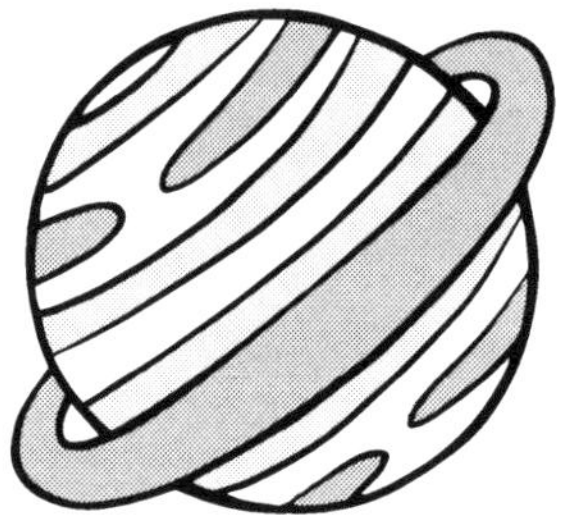

36. Did you know that **Mount Everes**t is **taller now** than the last time it was measured? It's not that the mountain has grown physically. Instead, the mountain is taller because of the movement in the Earth's tectonic plates.

37. The surface of **planet Mars** is covered in a lot of **iron oxide**. Iron oxide is the compound that gives a distinctive red color to **blood and rust** and it was named after the **Greek god of war**.

Fun Time

My new girlfriend is made of copper (Cu) and tellurium (Te) ??
I can now tell everyone she is really CuTe

38. **Gold and copper** are the **only non-silvery metals**. All other metals have a silvery appearance.

39. The **human body** is made of **billions and billions of atoms**, but the atoms are microscopic, and even then, **99%** of their composition is **empty space.**

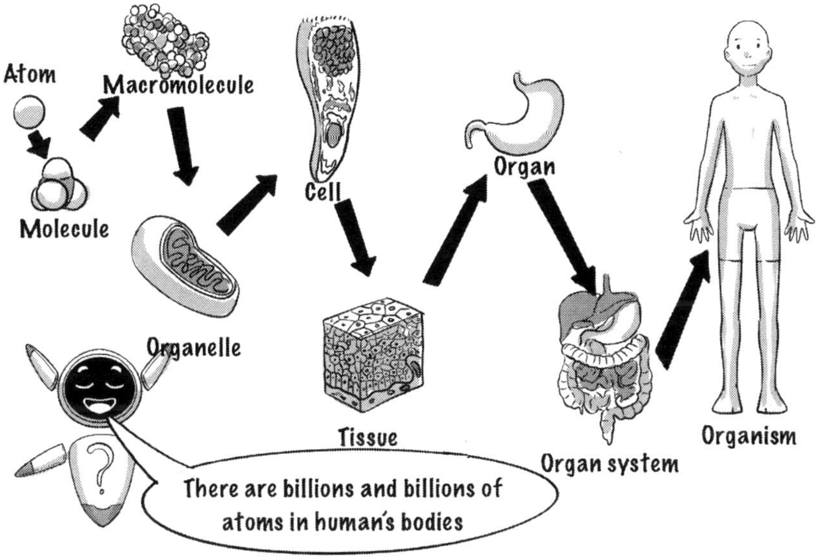

Fun Time

Name a five-letter word that means the same when you only keep the second and fourth letters.

Empty

40. If all these spaces were to be removed from the atoms,they would be so small. For this reason, scientists believeif all the spaces were to be removed, all the atoms fromall living human beings would fit into a spoon.

41. You can only burn a diamond with temperatures that exceed 1,000 degrees Celsius. Remember not to try this at home; it's not worth the time and energy. After all, you wouldn't be able to find this type of flame around,anyway.

42. The human body is made up of phosphorus, hydrogen, oxygen, nitrogen, calcium, and carbon, which are the most common. The less common elements are Sodium, Sulphur, potassium, chlorine, and magnesium.

If all these elements were to be removed and sold, theywould be just a little over $1. So, in the end, our worth is based on our virtues and knowledge rather than our body elements.

Fun Time

What did the shopkeeper say when he saw oxygen, hydrogen, sulfur, sodium, and phosphorus walking towards his shop?

OH SNaP

43. Carbon is the most abundant molecule in the human body after oxygen. If all the carbon in your body were removed, it would be enough to make 1000 pencils. Carbon is also one of the most abundant elements on the planet.

Fun Time

Why did carbon (C), Arsenic (As), and hydrogen (H) visit a bank?
They wanted to get some CAsH

44. Electric eels can produce electric shock as great as 500 volts. They do this to either hunt or for self-defense when they feel threatened.

45. Did you know that small insects such as the water strider can actually walk on water? This is because these insects are so light that their weight cannot penetrate the water surface.

46. Because the Amazon Forest produces up to 20% of the world's oxygen, many experts describe it as our planet's lungs.

47. Water will always feel cooler, even if it is the same temperature as the air. This is because water is a better conductor of heat than air. Air molecules are further apart, and thermal energy cannot transfer easily from one molecule to another, like water molecules. That's why water coolers are sometimes used on gaming computer CPUs and nuclear reactors.

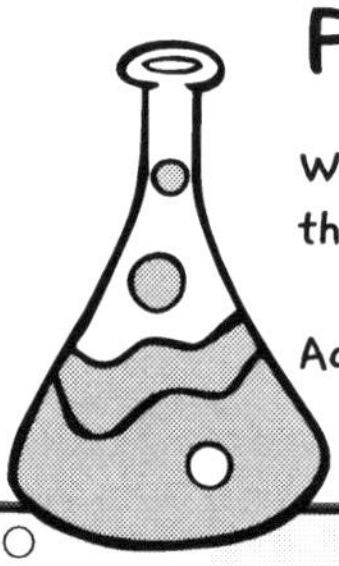

Fun Time

Wind: Water, I have noticed you never laugh at my jokes even though everyone else does. Why is that?

Aater: Sorry, Wind. I am just not a fan of dry humor.

48. The game of chess has more moves than all the atoms in the universe.

Those ways were discovered by Claude Shanon, who also wrote the first paper on how to program a computer to play chess. Unfortunately, it is hard to remember all the possible moves in this game, making it more about strategies. So, if you want to be an excellent strategist, then you should work on your chess skills.

49. The first thermometer was invented in the 1600s. It was called a thermoscope then.

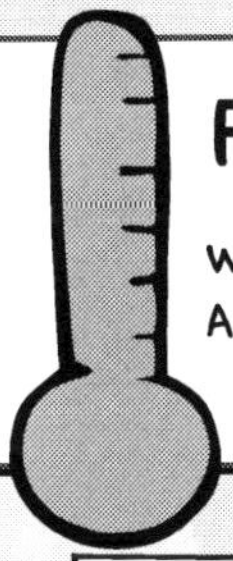

Fun Time

Which is smarter: a thermometer or a graduated cylinder?
A thermometer. It has lots of degrees.

50. You cannot freeze helium by cooling it to a temperature of zero like you would with water. The only way to freeze helium is to apply extreme pressure to it. This is because the gas molecules are so far apart that you need to bring them together using extreme pressure to freeze and condense them to solid.

Fun Time

I dropped two isotopes of helium on the floor in my Chemistry class last week.

All the teacher could say was He He.

51. As light enters a denser medium (like water or glass), its speed reduces, but the frequency remains constant. That's because, in a denser medium, there are extra particles that are blocking its path. So now you know how to reduce the speed of light!

52. There is a complex chemical process that can transform lead to gold. The process is called nuclear transmutation. So it is possible, but the process is so complex, it isn't worth the economic value of the resulting gold.

53. Why do we put salt on icy roads? Salt interrupts the water crystallization process that results in ice formation by lowering the freezing point of the water.

54. Did you know that Olympic gold medals are not made of pure gold? If anything, the gold medal contains more silver than gold. So the medal has 95% silver with roughly 6g of gold.

Fun Time

I stayed in a football stadium after the game was over last week and wondered why it was so hot.

Then I realized it was because all the fans had left.

They only add enough gold to make the medal have the characteristics of gold – like that golden color. The medal is worth no more than $550, while the bronze medal, having been made of zinc and copper, is equivalent to $3.5. Remember, the real value of the medal is in the accomplishment, hard work, persistence, worldwide and worldwide recognition.

55. Capsaicin is the molecule that gives peppers their hot nature. Birds lack the receptors needed to perceive the burning effect of hot peppers. For this reason, birds do not feel the burning sensation of pepper-like human beings, and other animals do.

56. Your stomach contains a mixture of acids strong enough to melt metal. If the strong combination of hydrochloric acid, potassium chloride, and sodium chloride fell on your skin, it would burn a hole right through it. It is a mind-blowing miracle that we walk around with high levels of acids in our bodies every day.

If you happen to throw up and it gets in the way and comes into contact with your precious necklace, then you must clean the necklace immediately. If you don't, the acidic contents from the stomach will quickly discolor the necklace.

Fun Time

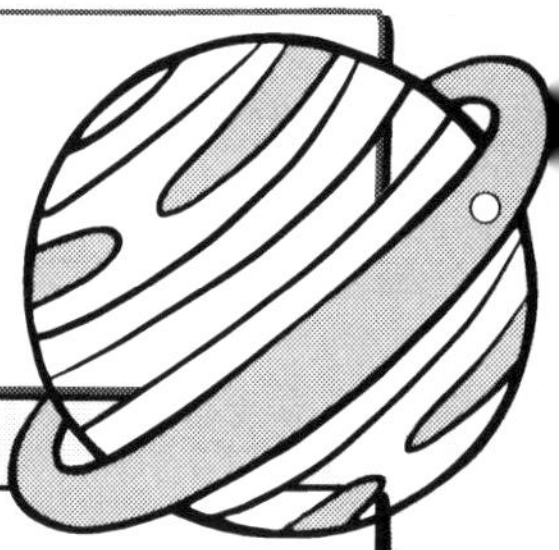

If the Earth and Mars go on holiday together, do you think they will leave the planet early?

57. Gold is super-flexible. A single ounce of the metal can be elongated to make up to 80km of wire. On the other hand, the wire would be so thin it would measure just 5 microns. That's why alloys are usually added to pure gold to make it more solid.

When you hear of the different versions of gold, such as 24, 18, and 16, always remember that the higher the number, the more gold there is in the object. So, for example, 24 contains more gold than 16 and 18.

58. The lightest and most common element found in the universe is hydrogen.

59. The oils cause the metallic smells found in coins from the human body. When oils from the human body come into contact with coins and other metals, they release this smell upon decomposition.

Fun Time

I spent ages wondering why all coins looked the same.
As I could not find the answer, I guess it is just a coincidence.

60. Osmium is the heaviest element that ever existed in terms of its density.

61. Did you know that the least acidic acid is the most dangerous? It is highly corrosive, and it can easily dissolve glass. It can be fatal when swallowed or even breathed. This acid is called hydrofluoric acid.

62. Diamond is the hardest material found on the surface of the Earth. The pressure and heat applied to diamondsmake their atoms crystallize in a very hard shape that's hard tobreak. That's why diamonds are used to cut other stones,glass, and even drill oil wells.

Fun Time

I do not know why my wife is so angry with me. It was our anniversary, and I took her to a baseball game.

After all, she did tell me she wanted to see a "huge diamond."

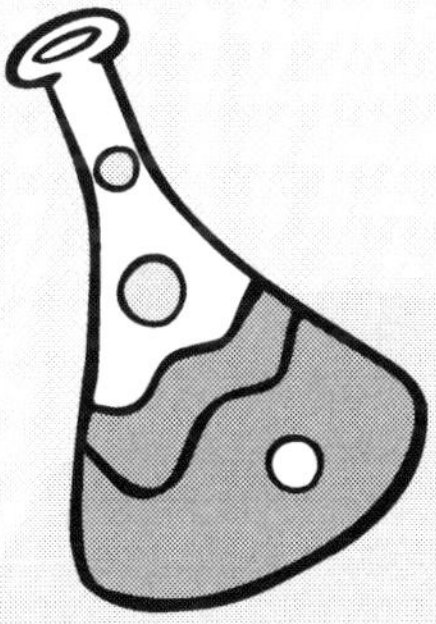

63. If you mix half a liter of water with half a liter of alcohol, the volume of the resulting liquid will be less than one liter. This is because the molecules of water and alcohol have different sizes. Alcohol has smaller particles that fall in between the spaces left by the water molecules.

This scenario is similar to mixing one liter of rocks and one liter of sand. The sand particles will fall between the rocks making the total volume of the mixture less than two liters.

64. The number of atoms in a single bucket of water is more than the total number of buckets of water needed to fill the Atlantic Ocean.

65. Did you know that Uranus is full of Methane and hydrogen, two highly flammable gases, but it doesn't burn? That's because oxygen is required for combustion to take place. Uranus lacks enough oxygen for the two flammable gases to burn.

66. Helium is lighter than air, and that's exactly why helium balloons float.

67. Why do people say the sunburns and yet it has no oxygen? The surface of the sun is full of hydrogen, which is a highly flammable gas, but the sun, just like Uranus, lacks enough oxygen for the hydrogen to burn.

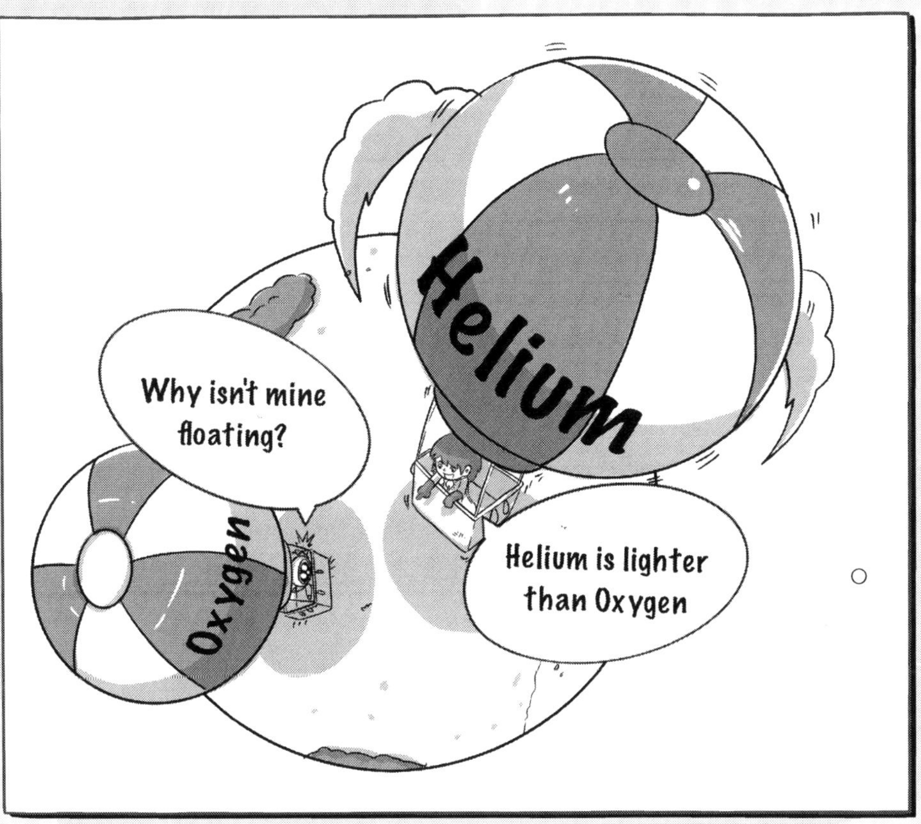

Fun Time

What were the sun' s first words to the Earth after there had been an eclipse?

I am pleased to heat from you again.

The truth is the sun is not really on fire; it doesn't burn. Instead, the heat light and heat from the sun come from the nuclear fusion of hydrogen and helium, a process that requires no oxygen.

68. Frozen carbon dioxide is also known as dry ice. That's because its surface temperature is -78 degrees Celsius.

69. Diamond is a pure form of carbon, so you might think that it may burn to produce carbon dioxide in the presence of oxygen. But this isn't the case. The structure of diamond is so tight and almost impossible to disrupt. That's why you can't burn a diamond.

70. 98% of all matter in the universe is made up of helium and hydrogen.

71. Did you know that different salts and metals are used to produce multiple-colored fireworks? For example, redf ireworks are produced by lithium salts. Gold and yellow colors are produced by iron. White is formed by magnesium.

Fun Time

Why are bullets and fireworks unhappy?

They only do their job properly after they have been fired.

72. Fatty acids are used to make basic soaps. The fatty acid is called stearic acid, and it is responsible for the lather and hardness of soap.

73. The softest material found on Earth is called Talc.

74. The venom from wasp and bee stings causes lots of pain. That's because the enzyme in the venom breaks down our cells which then causes the burning. Also, wasp stings are alkaline, but bee stings are acidic. So if you get stung, you need to put bicarbonate of soda (baking soda) on a bee sting and vinegar on a wasp sting. So pay attention to what stung you.

Fun Time

Boy Bee: Mum, why are you always so angry with me?
Mum Bee: because you never ever bee-hive yourself, that' s why!

75. Did you know that chemical processes have been in existence since 1000 BC? Back in the day, the processwas called alchemy. Alchemy was mostly developed totransfer copper to gold. During one ofthese processes, one Persian scientist called Zakaria Razidiscovered alcohol a little over a century ago.

76. Our planet has an estimated 170,000 tons of metric gold.

77. Water is not colorless. Even pure water with no impurities is not colorless. Water had a little blue color to it. Ocean water appears blue because it filters out the blue colors in the visible light spectrum while absorbing the red colors in the visible light spectrum.

Other particles in the water, such as plants or rocks, may reflect light and make the ocean water green or red.

Fun Time

What do oceans do when they see another ocean?
They give it a wave.

78. The speed of sound is four times faster in water than it is on land. That's because water molecules, unlike the air molecules on land, are closer to each other, which helps transmit the sound faster through the waves.

Fun Time

Did you know that water always travels quickly?
Because it always runs and never walks?

79. Your voice will have a higher pitch if you inhale helium. This is because helium makes the voice from your vocal cords travel faster.

80. Dimitri Mendeleev was a Russian scientist who created the periodic table. Unfortunately, his framework left gaps for undiscovered elements. With his invention, scientists were able to understand and predict the other elements that he had not included in his original periodic table.

81. Your pee would turn to gas and evaporate immediately if you peed in space. This is because space has no air pressure.

82. Enamel is the hardest chemical in the human body. It is the outer layer of tissue that coats teeth.

Fun Time

Why should you never be afraid of a comb?
Because even though it has teeth, it can never bite you.

83. Frogs don't need to drink water, even though they lovewater. Instead, they absorb moisture from the atmosphere through their skin.

Fun Time

Why should you never upset a frog? Because a frog eats whatever bugs it.

84. Did you know the temperature of lightning can exceed 30,000 degrees Celsius? That is five times as hot as the surface of the sun.

85. Huge icebergs can easily float on the ocean because ice is less dense than water.

86. The universe is made of two main things; matter and energy.

87. Electrons can move in waves or straight lines.

88. The speed of wind in high-altitude areas is much faster than the speed of wind in low-altitude areas such as oceans and seas.

89. Air has weight. The same level of accuracy used to weigh lead, iron, and any other type of solid material can be used to measure air.

90. Electromagnetic waves have both magnetic and electric fields. They don't need matter (air or water) to transfer. They can go across galaxies. They have different speeds, frequencies, and wavelengths.

Fun Time

My friend John did not need much time to finish his research on electromagnetic radiation. In fact, he said it was a pretty light subject.

91. The most important electromagnetic wave is light, without which we would be unable to see anything.

92. Radio waves have the longest wavelengths and which means they have very low frequency. Therefore, radio waves are quite helpful in receiving and sending information.They have mostly used satellites, the internet, sonar,radar, radio, and the world wide web.

93. The remote control uses infrared waves to send signals to the television.

Fun Time

What do cows do in their free time?
They listen to moo-sic and visit moo-seums.

94. Microwaves are quite short, and they are used in weather forecasting, microwave ovens, and receiving and sending information.

95. Velocity and speed are two different forms of energy in physics. Speed refers to how fast an object is moving, while velocity refers to how fast an object is moving in a specific direction.

96. Temperature is a description of how fast or slow the atoms and molecules inside an object are moving. A high temperature means the atoms and molecules are moving at high speed and vice versa.

Fun Time

I live next door to an atom, but I never believe a single word he says.

I know he makes up everything.

If 23 people are sitting in a single room, the chances of two of them sharing a birthday are 50%. Even more mind-blowing is the fact that there is a 99% chance of two people sharing a birthday if 75 people are sitting in a room.

This phenomenon is called the Birthday Paradox, and it is derived from the complex mathematical theory of compounding the power of exponents.

Chemistry & Physics Jokes

Does anyone know any jokes about sodium?
Na!

What did the scientists say whey they found two isotopes of helium
HeHe!

What do you do with a dead chemist
Barium!

What’ s a sign of a lousy chemistry joke?
No reaction

How often does a chemist need coffee?
They need caffeine periodically.

What do you call an acid with a bad attitude
A-mean-o-acid

What do you say when someone throws sodium chloride at you?
That's salt!

One acid said to the other.
You are overreacting!

There is a DJ called DJ Enzymes.
He is always breaking it down!

CHAPTER 5: EARTH SCIENCE

Earth is an amazing place that is home to a wide variety of plants, animals, and even human beings themselves. Earth combines the beauty of oceans, seasons, jungles, and atmospheres into a single element that works perfectly. It is the only planet that has life on it.

Fun Time

Mike: You know, even though it is 22 April (Earth Day), I am still really tired after such a long March.

Scientists are still searching and studying other planets to see if there are any that can support life, like Earth.

Fun Time

You know, it really makes my days when I watch the Earth rotate.

Here are some fun facts about deserts, oceans, dinosaurs, and all other interesting things on our planet.

Dinosaurs

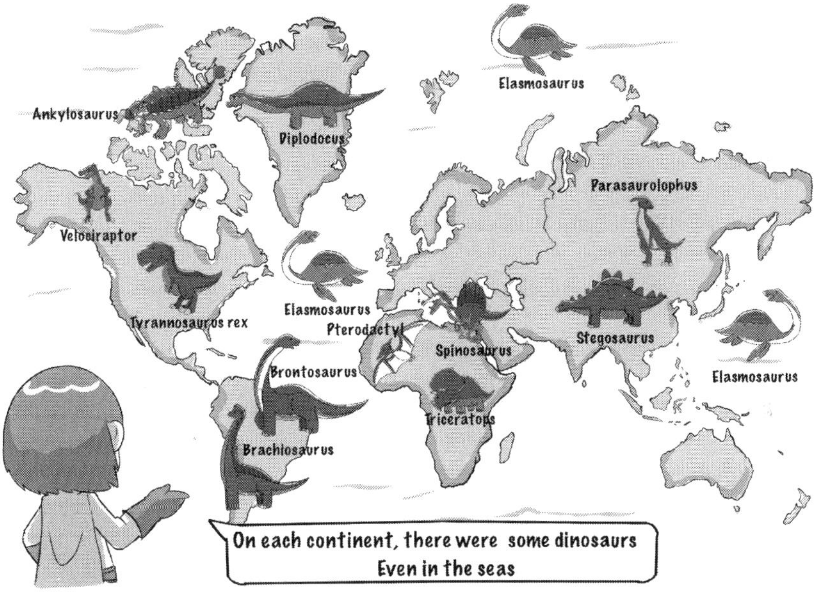

Dinosaurs are a group of reptiles that walked the Earth millions of years ago. Not only were they strange, but some of them were super-huge and powerful, while others were small and hunted in packs. They are still a subject of research to this day, and other species are still being discovered. For this reason, dinosaurs are fascinating animals to everyone.

Fun Time

Q: If you see a dinosaur, you will always see something following it. Do you know what it is?

A: Its tail

1. Richard Owens, a British paleontologist (a person who studies fossils), invented the word dinosaur. He came up with the name from two Greek words, "dienos" and "saurus" which mean terrible and reptile, respectively when translated.

2. All animals are grouped as either warm or cold-blooded. Dinosaurs, however, were neither cold nor warm-blooded. Therefore, they are classified as in between cold and warm.

3. Human beings have occupied the Earth for about 2.5 million years, while scientists report that dinosaurs occupied the Earth more than 160 million years ago. This is approximately 64 times as long as humans have existed.

4. Scientists agree that dinosaurs are the largest animals ever existed. Some of them had tails as long as 45 feet. The tails helped them keep their balance while they were running. This is not to generalize all the dinosaurs because some were human-sized, and others were even smaller.

Fun Time

I watched some dinosaurs play American football last week. It was a bit boring until a tyrannosaurus dino scored in the second period.

5. They may look scary, but the **biggest dinosaurs** only ate plants. In fact, most of them were herbivorous. Plant-eating dinosaurs were very greedy. They ate large amounts of food. Some even swallowed branches and leaves without chewing, and this is why they were so huge.

6. Can you pronounce the word **Micropachycephalosaurus**? Well, this 23-letter word is the name of a dinosaur species that was discovered in China. It means "a thick-headed, small reptile".

Fun Time

Q. What did the dinosaur buy at the hardware store?
A. Some rep-tiles for his kitchen floor

7. Fossils of dinosaurs have been found on all continents including Antarctica. Scientists, therefore, believe that dinosaurs lived on all continents.

8. Tyrannosaurus Rex **(T-rex)** is believed to be one of the most violent and brutal dinosaurs. Its bite was twice as powerful as a lion's, and it was as big as a school bus.

Fun Time

What is the difference between a bus and a cycle?

A bus stand does not go along with the bus, but a cycle stand goes with the cycle.

9. Dinosaurs differed greatly from each other. Some walked on **four legs** while others walked on two. Some had developed attack mechanisms such as spikes and horns, while others developed a thick skin for protection. Some dinosaurs had feathers, just like birds do today. Dinosaurs evolved based on their needs and environment to survive.

10. The **largest** dinosaur weighed **77 tons**. That's equal to 17 African elephants combined. This dinosaur was called **Argentinosaurus**, and it is also the longest and largest land animal to have existed. The remains of this dinosaur were found in Argentina, South America.

11. **Archelon** is a type of **turtle** that no longer exists. The late Cretaceous is the largest turtle ever to have been discovered, with the biggest one measuring **460 cm (15 ft)**from head to tail, **400 cm (13 ft)** from flipper to flipper, and2,200 kg (4,900 lb) in weight.

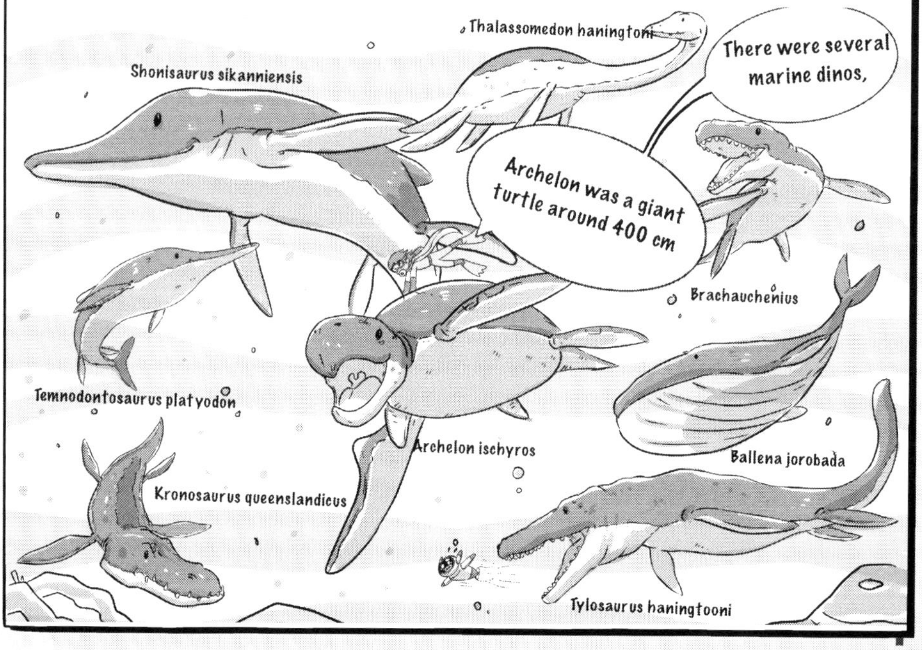

Fun Time

Mummy Brain: Come on, Baby Brain. Time for your bath.
Baby Brain: No! If I go in the bath, I will be brainwashed.

12. As huge as some of them were, dinosaurs had tiny brains. Even the brain of a newborn child is bigger than that of a full-grown adult dinosaur. However, the winner for this category was the Stegosaurus, whose brain was the size of a walnut. Its brain measured only **3 centimeters** long with a weight of **75 grams**. Scientists believe that the smartest dinosaurs were probably the small meat-eating ones.

13. **Dinosaurs' eggs** came in multiple sizes. The smallest one discovered so far measured only 0.7 inches, no more than the diameter of a penny, while the biggest egg measured 19 inches **(48.26 centimeters)** long, that's around the size of a rugby ball.

14. **Megalosaurus was the first officially named dinosaur. Reverend William Buckland named it in 1974.**

15. **Most dinosaurs that ate meat walked on two feet. Withtwo feet on the ground and the other modi f ied into hand-l ike features, they could run very fast and catch prey with their "hands".**

Fun Time

What did the dinosaur say to the server in a restaurant?
Can I have some dino-sauce for my steak?

16. Most **plant-eating** dinosaurs travelled around in groups for safety purposes. Their trampling left paths as big as "superhighways" behind. One of these highways was discovered in **China** in 2001. Some plant-eating animals, such as zebras, buffaloes, and wildebeests, etc., still use this strategy for safety.

Fun Time

Did you know zebras are so old they can still only be seen in black and white?

17. Roy Chapman, an American explorer, was the first person to discover dinosaur eggs. This happened in 1923 in the Mongolian Desert. Before his discovery, scientists didn't know what dinosaur eggs looked like.

18. One of the biggest examples found was a **Mosasaurus Hoffmanni** and was guessed to be about **56 feet (17 meters)** long in life, according to a 2014 study that appeared in the journal Proceedings of the Zoological Institute RAS. Not all mosasaurs were giants, though.

19. The first dinosaur remains were discovered by a scientist called Ferdinand Vandiveer Hayden in 1854. The remains were found in North America on the Upper Missouri River.

20. Dinosaur **skulls** had big holes. These holes were meant to keep them cool and make their heads lighter.

Fun Time

What does a dinosaur do while he is sleeping?
He dino-snores

21. Most scientists believe that birds may have evolved from dinosaurs, especially the beast-footed dinosaurs known as **theropods**. Some dinosaurs were even known to have feathers.

22. Scientists have discovered that the bones of meat-eating dinosaurs were full of air. The bones were huge but certainly not as heavy as most of us believe. Birds have hollow bones, too, which make them lighter for flight.

Fun Time

Jack: Last night, I saw my scientist neighbor taking out his doorbell. Why do you think he would do that?

Penny: I heard he was hoping to win a no-bell prize!

Animals

1. Did you know that there are no female and male **Earthworms**? A single Earthworm has **both female and male** reproductive organs.

2. Just like human beings have **fingerprints**, gorillas have **nose prints.** The **wrinkle pattern** found on their nose is unique to each one of them. Conservation workers keep track of individual gorillas by observing their nose prints on sketches and photos.

3. **Giraffes** have **seven bones** in their necks, just like humans do. The only difference is that giraffe bones are much **larger**.

4. **Whales** and **dolphins** are aquatic mammals (mammals that live in the water), but they are the closest relatives of **hippos**.

Fun Time

Q: Where do hippopotami apply to when they want to become Doctors?
A: A hippocampus.

5. The **tongue** of a **chameleon** is as long as its body. This helps them grab insects super-fast – within a fraction of a second. Can you imagine having a tongue as long as your body?

6. The **eyesight** of an **eagle** is four times as sharp as that of humans. As a result, they can see objects from very high up in the sky.

Fun Time

Q. Of all the birds in the sky, which one is most in need of a wig?
A. Bald eagle!

7. Did you know that **huskies** can run for hours and hours? They can endure long races for long periods going at speeds of **31km** per hour **(20m/hr)**. They are used as sled dogs which help with sled transportation.

8. A **starfish** will still survive if it is split into five different pieces as long as every piece contains a small portion of the central disk. Then, it can regrow to a whole starfish again.

Fun Time

Alice: I have just bought a fish with no eye?
Molly: And does this fish have a name?
Alice: Yes, I call it fsh

9. **Hummingbirds** can flap their wings as fast as **200 times** per second to hover around.

10. Did you know that when a **nine-banded armadillo** gets pregnant, it will most likely give birth to four identical babies? Imagine having four **identical babies**. How do you tell the difference between each of them?

11. A jaguar's eyesight is six times as good as that of a human being in the dark.

12. The antlers of **reindeers** have a velvety covering when they are still growing. When the antlers mature, the **velvet** covering falls off.

13. **Tortoises** found in the **Galapagos Islands** near Ecuador are super huge. Some of them weigh as much as brown bears – 250kgs (550lbs). Tortoises are amongst the oldest animals on Earth also.

14. The **lifespan** of a female **housefly** lasts just a few days. However, she can lay up to **500 eggs** during that period with an average of 100-150 eggs every day.

Fun Time

Comedians love eggs because every time you tell them a joke they crack up.

15. Are you familiar with the **"twit-twoo"** sounds of **tawny owls**? The sounds are made by a female and male pair. The female's call is the "twit," and the male replies with a "twoo" sound that sounds like a hooting.

16. **Sea otters** have the **thickest fur** in the mammalian kingdom. Large males can have up to 800 million hairs when humans only have 500 million hairs.

17. Did you know that **fleas** from cats can **jump** as high as **60 times** their body length? So it seems like they are very good gymnasts, right?

18. The **roar** of a **lion** is the loudest of all the big cats. A lion's roar can be heard as far as **5 kilometers** (3 miles) away.

Fun Time

Q: What did the lion say when he met the deer?
A: Hello. It' s a pleasure to eat you.

19. **Pigeons** have a rare ability. Both the males and females produce **"crop milk,"** a substance used to feed their young ones. Only doves, pigeons, penguins, and flamingos have this unique ability.

20. **Emperor penguins** can dive as far as **500m deep** and stay underwater for around 27 minutes. They may look slow and funny on land, but they are very agile and fast swimmers in the water. They are also excellent fish hunters.

21. **Human** beings share **98.8%** of **chimpanzee DNA.** This difference may seem small, but in reality, it is not. There are 35 million differences between humans and chimpanzees.

22. Two-humped **camels**, also known as **Bactrians**, drink up to **50 liters of water** in a single sitting. They can then go for months without having to drink water again.

23. Did you know that **kiwis**, unlike other **birds**, have **nostrils** at the very end of their long beaks? Again, Kiwis in New Zealand forage at night.

24. There are more than **470 shark species**, and they have been in existence for over 400 million years. The average lifespan of a shark is **25 years**, but it can live for 100 years.

25. Were you aware that **sharks** don't have any **bones**? Instead, their skeletons are made of a substance called cartilage.

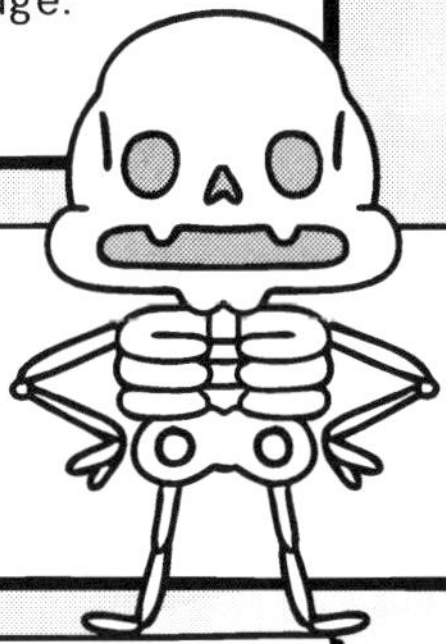

Fun Time

What instrument does the skeleton play?
The trom-bone.

19. The eye of an **ostrich** is bigger than its **brain**.

27. **Hummingbirds** are generally known to be super small, but did you know that the **bee hummingbirds** are so tiny that they are frequently mistaken insects?
Bee's hummingbirds are the smallest birds in the world. They measure an average of 2 ½ inches only with a weight no more than a dime.

Fun Time

Q. Bob: Hummingbird, why are you humming?
A. Hummingbird: I am sorry, but I don' t know the words.

28. **Wood frogs** found in **Alaska** can hold their pee for up to eight months. However, they hold their urine during the cold winter months and only relieve themselves in the warm summer months. This is because **special microbes** in the frog's gut recycle the urea found in their urine into nitrogen during those months.

29. There are an estimated **8.7 million** species of **animals** and plants on Earth. Yet, human beings have dominated the world. We have built big cities and are well advanced in technology, but we are just a single drop in the ocean of all living things on our beautiful planet.

Jokes About Animals

Sally: Maggie, my dog has just chewed my dictionary. What should I do?
Maggie: You should take the words out of her mouth.

Q. If you need a dog that will help you be on time, what dog would you get?
A. A watchdog, of course!

Q. Why don' t leopards like playing hide and seek?
A. They are always spotted first.

Oceans

1. Did you know that starfish can be born square? This is a very rare birth disorder that the fish is born with, and scientists still don't know what causes this to happen.

2. Sharks have the longest pregnancies in the world -- up to 42 months. Sharks are being killed by pollution, illegal fishing, and by-catching, mostly perpetrated by human beings. A recent study reported that every year 100 million sharks are killed by human beings.

Fun Time

If you go fishing with a librarian, you will always notice that they put bookworms on the end of their line.

3. **Oceans** cover most of the **Earth's surface**. In fact, they cover **71%** of it. However, when these oceans are combined with underground water bodies, the total coverage shoots up to 99.9%.

4. Scientists have successfully mapped just a little over **5%** of the **seafloor**. In fact, we are more familiar with the surface of the moon than the ocean floors.

5. Oceans are super **deep**. The deepest point measures **10,994 meters down**, and it is found in the Mariana Trench. Mount Everest could fit in this trench, and its tallest peak would still be a few miles below the surface of the water.

Fun Time

Q. Which creature in the ocean do the other creatures not want to fight with?

A. The mussels

6. The largest ocean in the world is the **Pacific Ocean**. At its widest, it exceeds the diameter of the moon up to 5 times. The Pacific Ocean also has a total of **25,000 islands**.

7. The ocean is full of valuable **treasures**. Scientists believe that the oceans have more valuable items than all the museums in the world combined. For example, an estimated more than 3 million **shipwrecks**, each with millions worth of historical treasures, are found on the ocean floor. Experts also believe that there are almost **20 million tonne**s of **gold** dissolved in seawater. This is enough gold for all of us to have at least 9 pounds!

Fun Time

Q. Every time the ocean meets the shore, what does it say?
A. It doesn't say anything. It just gives it a wave.

8. Did you know that over **half of** the **USA** is actually in the ocean? That's because of all the island territories, the Alaskan peninsula, and the long coastlines.

9. Ahmed Gabr set the world record for the longest **scuba dive** in 2014. He went as deep as **332.5 meters** in the **Red Sea**, and this took him just 12 minutes. The ascent was much deeper, though; it took him 15 hours to safely get back to the surface.

It could be fatal if a diver tries to come back to the surface very fast after a deep dive. This is because they can suffer from air or gas embolism. This is where an air bubble gets trapped in the blood vessel and blocks it.

Fun Time

Do you know why I quit my job as a scuba diver? Because I was under lots of pressure.

Nitrogen bubbles can form inside the blood vessels and may also
get sucked into the bloodstream through the arteries resulting in
10. heart attack, stroke, and even death.

Call for help or an ambulance as soon as you realize someone is feeling unwell after scuba diving.

Fun Time

Q. What does the sea use as Christmas decorations?
A. Coral reefs

11. The largest **waterfall** in the world is in the ocean. It is an **underwater waterfall** called Denmark Strait Cataract, and it is found between Iceland and Greenland. The water flows at a rate of 123 million cubic feet per second. That's at least 50,000 times the rate of water flow in Niagara Falls.

Fun Time

Q. What is the opposite of a firefly?
A. A waterfall

12. Did you know that a single **iceberg** can provide **one million** people with enough **water** to drink for five years? Antarctica has icebergs that are so big; they contain up to 20 million gallons of water.

13. **Oceans** are like a completely different world. They have **lakes**, **mountains**, **volcanoes**, and even rivers. As the water flows into the ocean, it creates depressions that look like the lakes we know.

14. Did you know that there is a **jellyfish** species that can **never die**? So it looks like immortality is not just a thing of our dreams. Scientists have realized that the **Turritopsis dohrnii** jellyfish can return to its initial life stages and continue its life cycle endlessly.

15. **Coral reefs** support up to **25%** of known **marine species**. This means that they, in turn, provide income, medicine, and food to millions of people worldwide. The yearly estimated value of coral reefs is about **$30 billion,** and yet experts still believe that this is an underestimation.

16. **Mongolia** is a land-locked country. Therefore, there is no need for them to have a **Navy**, but they still want it anyway. For this reason, the **Mongolian Navy** is made up of a single **tugboat** with a **seven-man crew**. Of the seven men, only a single one knows how to swim.

17. **Hippos** are enormous, but did you know they lack **sweat glands**? Instead, they use mucus glands that secrete an oily substance that turns orange-red in the sun. It is called **"blood sweat".**

Fun Time

Can you name the animal's name when you cross a hippo with an elephant and a rhinoceros?

Helephino

18. **Seawater** is not drinkable, but did you know that **sea ice** is actually **drinkable**? This is not to say that it is safe to drink sea ice directly from the sea, but it becomes fresh enough for human consumption during the ice ages.

19. Did you know that **volcanic eruptions** (mountains produce gas and lava) happen in the **seas** and **oceans**? In fact, **90%** of volcanic activity is believed to happen there. The South Pacific has the highest number of volcanic activities – a total of 1,133 volcanoes.

20. Great **white sharks** have **thousands of teeth**. They can lose up to **20,000 teeth** in their lifetime. However, they will have at least 300 teeth and regrow them constantly throughout their life.

21. Did you know that the **blood** of **octopuses** is **blue**? Did you know they have three hearts? This is very interesting, but their blood is blue because it contains copper instead of iron.

Fun Time

Q. How do you know an octopus is on the toilet?
A. The sign on the door says octopied.

22. Have you ever heard of the **Killer Whale** (Orca)? Well, it turns out that this name is quite misleading because this "whale" is actually a species of **dolphin**.

23. Water **lilies** in the Amazon can grow as big as **6 feet** (1.8 meters) wide. So that's probably taller than you, right?

24. **Bamboos** grow very fast. Some species can grow up to **91 cm in a single day**.

25. Earth's surface is covered by 70% of water.

26. The **Mariana Trench** is the **deepest** ocean point known to human beings. It is found in the Pacific Ocean; it is semi-circle in shape with an approximate length of **2,550km** (1584.497miles) and a width of 69 km (42.8746 miles)

Fun Time

Q. Who do all the sea creatures ask to clean the ocean?
A. Mermaids

27. Did you know that some **fish cough**, just like we do? They do this to clear bacteria and particles from their gills.

27. Dolphins are really smart animals. When they sleep, only half of their brain sleeps while the other half stays alert.

Fun Time

Do you know that goldfish weren' t always orange. But over time, the water made them rusty.

26. Did you know that the **heart** of a **shrimp** is found on its **head**?

27. **Sharks** do not consider humans as prey. They only attack human beings when they are hunting for **human-sized prey**, seals, and dolphins. It is usually a case of mistaken identity.

Deserts

1. Did you know that over **one billion** people live in **deserts**? With the water scarcity, hot temperatures, and dangerous animals, life in desert regions is genuinely challenging, but some communities have adapted to it.

2. All the seven continents in the world have desertes. Even **Antarctica** itself is a vast **ice desert.** Up to 1/3 of the Earth's surface is made up of desert areas. That's around **20.9 million square miles** of the Earth's surface.

3. There is so much **life in the deserts**. If anything, the amount of life in the deserts comes close to the kind of life in the rainforests. Experts believe that up to **200 rattlesnakes** can exist comfortably in a **single square mile** of the Sonoran Desert.

Fun Time

Q. What subject do snakes love when at school?
A. Hiss-story

4. Many **desert animals** are **nocturnal**. This means that they sleep during the day and only come out **during the night**. At night it is cooler, making it easier for them to roam about.

5. Every desert in the world has a different climate. For example, **coastal deserts** have **warm summers** and cool winters, while **dry deserts** have very hot summers and warm all-year weather.

Fun Time

Ben: Jessie, did you know that it started raining MONEY yesterday?

Jessie: Well, the weatherman did say there would be a change in the weather.

6. The **tiniest desert** in the world is found in **Yukon, Canada**. It is called the **Carcross Desert**, and it measures just a single tiny square-inch mile.

7. The **largest** hot **desert** in the world is the **Sahara Desert.** In the summer, temperatures can rise to **122 degrees Celsius**.

Fun Time

Q. What does the Gobi desert say every time it meets someone?
A. Hello. Long time no sea!

8. The **Atacama Desert** is the **driest** in the world. with average rainfall of around 15 millimetres (0.6 inch) per year

Fun Time

What do you call the desert-related jokes?
Dry humor.

9. **Hiking**, **ATV bike rides,** and **rock climbing** are among the most popular tourist **activities** in the deserts.

10. Did you know that desert plants can live for more than 150 years? A good example is the Saguaro Cactus which can live for more than 100 years.

Jungle

Jungles are regions that overflow with thick forests, vegetation, and wild tangles.

1. Did you know that **jungles** cover **6%** of the **Earth's surface**?

Fun Time

Q. What animal would be you if you tried to copy other people' s answers in a test?

A. You would be a cheetah.

2. Jungles provide habitat for over **1,300** different bird species.

3. If all the **ants** on the jungle floor were combined, they would weigh four times as much **as all the mammals** living in the jungle.

Fun Time

Baby Ant: Mummy, there is one thing I am really confused about.
Mummy Ant: What' s that, baby ant?
Baby Any: Why are all my uncle' s ants?

4. **Rival strawberry dart frogs** that are found in the Central American rainforests can **wrestle** for over 20 minutes.

Fun Time

Q. What did the frog do when his car broke down?
A. he got it toad away.

5. Did you know that a **rainforest's canopy** is so thick that a raindrop can take up to **10 minutes to penetrate** it to reach the floor of the jungle?

6. There is a tribe in **New Guinea** called the **Korowai**. They live in tree houses as high as **45 meters above the ground**. How do their young ones get up there?

7. Up to ¼ **of ingredients** used in manufacturing **modern medicine** are extracted from **plants** in the world's rainforests.

8. **Australian** rainforests are very beautiful, and they have unique plants. **80% of their plants** are **not found** elsewhere in the world.

9. The A**mazon Forest** is so big, and if it was a country, it would be the **9th biggest country** in the world. However, it is located in South America.

Antarctica

1. Did you know that **90% of the world's ice** is found on the **Antarctica** continent? It also contains 70% of the world's freshwater.

2. **Antarctica** is the **5th largest continent** in the world. However, there is **no official language** there, it has no capital city, and no country in the world controls it.

Fun Time

It can be lonely living in Antarctica because it is hard to break the ice when you meet new people.

3. **Reptiles** might be **cold-blooded**, but they are **not found** in Antarctica. If anything, there are **warm-blooded** animals such as penguins living in Antarctica. The emperor penguin can even survive in Antarctica's harsh winters.

4. **Antarctica** is an **icy desert**. 9.8 inches of snow fall on its surface every year. The snow that is seen there is old, and it never melts.

Fun Time

Q. Why does Antarctica feel lonely?
A. Because it is so ice-O-lated.

5. A **single mass of ice sheet** covers **99% of Antarctica.** This ice sheet is the largest on the planet.

6. You don't need a **visa** to travel to **Antarctica**. You only need a passport. As it is, Antarctica is a surprisingly popular tourist destination. More than **40,000** people visit this continent every year.

Fun Time

Did you hear about the people with Covid in Antarctica
They are all in ice-olation

7. Antarctica is freezing cold. Even water vapor freezes and forms crystals up in the air. These frozen crystals are called **diamond dust**.

8. The **winds** in **Antarctica** can reach speeds of up to **200mph**. As a result, it is the windiest continent on Earth.

Fun Time

If a bear visits both the North Pole and Antarctica, would that make it a bipolar bear?

9. The first recorded **childbirth** was of a **baby Emile Marco Palma**. His mother was sent there by the **Argentinian** government in 1979 to claim a portion of the **Antarctica**.

10. **No trees** or shrubs grow in **Antarctica**.

CHAPTER 6: ENGINEERING

Imagine a world without internet, televisions, computers, or mobile phones. How hard would life be? Would you be able to access social media to watch funny videos or comment on your best friend's photos? Unfortunately, that would not be possible.

Worse than that, movies and computer games would be a thing of our dreams and fantasies, which is to say, life would be very dull.

Luckily, our world is modern. We've got advanced technology that makes life easier and more enjoyable - thanks to engineering.

Fun Time

While an optimist thinks a glass is half full and a pessimist thinks a glass is half empty, an engineer thinks it is twice as big as it needs to be.

The engineer: "the glass is twice as big as it needs to be."

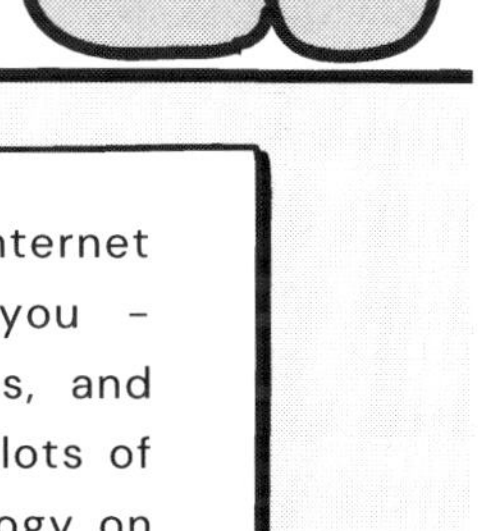

Engineering is the mastermind behind the existence of the internet and most of the fascinating things you see around you - superhighways, tall buildings, cars, televisions, smartphones, and other electronic gadgets. Isn't that cool? Engineers deserve lots of appreciation and respect, for they are the pillars of technology on planet earth.

Now, let's find out the general fun facts about engineering.

Fun Time

Mum: Brian, why on earth did you throw your watch out of the window?
Brian: Because dad always says time flies, so I wanted to actually see it.

1. **Levi Hutchins** was the first person to invent the **alarm clock** in **1787**, which could only ring at 4 AM. The reason was that Levi had made the alarm clock specifically for himself to wake him up for his job. That was until **1847** when a French inventor, **Antoine Redier**, designed an adjustable **mechanical alarm clock**.

2. It took a total of 8 long hours for the very **first photograph** ever taken to be exposed. The photograph was taken in **1826** and is known as the ***View from the Window at Le Gras***. By 1839, this exposure time was reduced to just 15 seconds. But, of course, it still doesn't work for smile-friendly photographs, right?

   Try doing this yourself and see how difficult it was. Set a timer for 15 minutes, stay perfectly still, and put a constant smile on your face. Wait until the timer goes off, and then take the picture. It's pretty exhausting, right?

Fun Time

Q: What is a lobster doing with a camera?
A: Taking a shellfie

You see, **need** is the mother of inventions, so next time you feel you need something and you can't find any product for it, that's an opportunity for a new million-dollar invention.

3. The direct invention that led to the modern **television** was invented in 1927 by a 21-years-old guy called **Philo Taylor Farnsworth.**

4. The radio took almost 38 years and television 15 years to reach 50 million users, but it only took **35 days** for the **Angry Birds Space** game to get to **50 million users.**

Fun Time

Q: Why did the radio station not allow a fish to be a DJ?
A: They said if he went on air, he would die.

5. While the term "**robot**" makes you think of a complicated machine, it originates from a simple Czech term, "**robota**," which means "**forced labor**".

6. Do you love trains? If so, you'll be intrigued to hear this. In the 18th century, the **first train** on Earth traveled at less than **10 miles per hour**. But due to how fast technology is advancing today, trains can travel thirty times faster. That is, some trains have over 300 miles per hour top speed. Superfast, right?

Fun Time

Q: How do teachers and trains differ?
A: Teachers will tell you to "spit the gum out", while trains will tell you to "chew chew' '

7. If you're planning to give up on anything, wait till you hear this. **Thomas Edison,** the person who invented the **light bulb**, failed 1000 times before succeeding. So imagine if he had given up. Then, maybe, we wouldn't be talking of bulbs right now, or the invention would have taken longer.

8. Mechanical engineer **Karl Benz** made the **first automobile** (the old-times car) in Germany in 1886. Powered by a gasoline engine, the three-wheeled and two-seater automobile could reach a top speed of 16km/h (10 miles per hour)

Fun Time

Q. How do you know you are talking to an engineer?

A. He will try to solve a problem that you didn't know existed and do so in a way that you don't understand.

9. The fastest **roller coaster** can reach its top speed (150 miles per hour)in just **5 seconds**!

10. Imagine going to school in a car with no driver. Yeah, nodriver at all. It drops you ar school safe and sound before driving itself back home. How cool is that? Well, such cars exist but are still under testing. Engineers and scientists are working on them to ensure they are super safe to use forcommercial use.

11. You've probably seen a **Video Camera Recorder** and noticedthat it isn't that big. But when you compare the present-dayVideo Camera Recorder with the first one invented in 1956,the size can nearly scare you away. Its size was like that of apiano. A little too big to fit in a pocket and carry around.

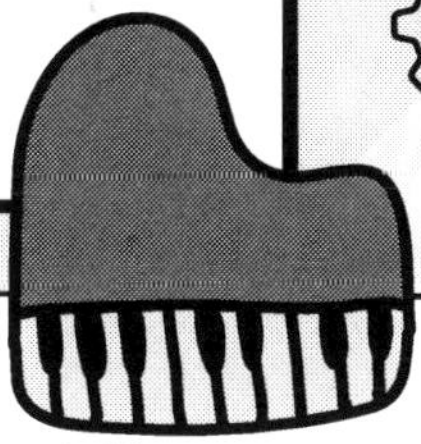

Fun Time

Q. Do you know why the pianist had problems opening the piano lid?
A. Because all the keys were inside.

12. Many people think that the **QWERTY** computer keyboard is designed to increase their typing speed. That's far from the truth. It's the opposite. When typewriters came to exist, typing quickly would jam the keys.

Therefore, the **QWERTY** keyboard was introduced (by Christopher Sholes in 1868) to slow down typing speed - by keeping standard alphabets far from each other. So maybe it's about time a new keyboard design was invented, don't you think so?

Fun Time

Q. Do you know why the pianist had problems opening the piano lid?
Q. Of all the keys on a keyboard, which one would an astronaut like best?
A. The space bar.

13. The tallest building in the world is called **Burj Khalifa**, located in Dubai. It's taller than you can ever imagine. It has a standing height of 828 meters and has 163 floors. That's just a few meters away from being a one-kilometer-high building.

And what's more, the building's design is beautiful, which increases its fame. Indeed, the civil engineers and the architects involved must have had sharp minds to develop such a tall and beautiful tower. Nevertheless, it took six years to build it.

14. Has it ever crossed your mind why your eyes dry out more often when using a computer? Here's the answer. As an average **computer user**, you blink **seven times a minute**, far less than the usual 20 times per minute. Therefore, your eyes become less moistened.

15. **Bi l l Gates**, the founder of one of the largest computer software companies, **Microsoft** , qui t school to pursue his dream of creating Microsoft's. However, he had a firm grasp of computer-related processes like hacking and coding.

In short, he had excellent computer skills and was obsessed with stuff related to technology. But why did he drop out? Simple. He dropped out to establish a world-known software company – Microsoft using his computer skills.

16. Can you believe that there was once a computer **powered bywater**? I t 's true. In 1936, **Vladimir Sergeevich** bui l t a computer that operated using water. The computer could solve complex math equat ions.

Fun Time

Q. Boss: Computer, why are you always late for work?
A. Computer: I have a hard drive.

17. Did you know that 86 % of computer users try to plug **USB devices** (like smartphone charger cables and flash)upside down on computers? Maybe you're one of them.

18. A cool guy called **Doug Engelbart** created the first **computer mouse** with a wooden casing in **1964**.

19. How small is 5MB of data? - hardly enough to store two photos from your smartphone's camera. Now check this. A **supercomputer** in the year **1956** (the 305 RAMAC from IBM) had a hard drive with a 5MB storage capacity and weighedover one ton. It was so heavy that even loading it on a plane required a forklift.

20. Do you know **Apple**, the company behind the famous **iPhone** smartphones? Their first logo featured **Isaac Newton** under atree, with an apple just about to hit his head.

Fun Time

Q: Do you know what comes after the USA (United States of America)?
A: Yep USB

21. If you can picture yourself as a **typist** (a guy behind the computer keyboard) in a company, your fingers can travel a distance of 12.6 miles on an average workday due to typing.

22. **Martin Cooper**, an engineer, made the first call using a handheld mobile phone from Motorola Company, on April 3, 1973. Interestingly, he called his rival (Joel Engel, an engineer in another company) to tell him that the **Motorola** company had invented the functional portable phone. What an excellent way to roast his business competitor.

23. **Nokia**, the company that was well-known for selling mobile phones, used to sell toilet paper. That's unbelievable to some extent, but here's the thing. When the company was established in 1865, it was a pulp mill (a factory that created papers, including tissues).

Fun Time

Sam: Penny, why do we still have a landline.

Penny: So we can look for our cell phone when we lose it.

Fun Time

Q: What did the lobster say when it answered the phone?
A: Shello.

24. **Nokia** entered the phone industry in the '80s. This shows that to survive, you must adapt to new technologies as they are invented. Unfortunately, Nokia didn't consider this fact later on when smartphones were invented, and other competitors such as Apple and Samsung quickly took their place in the market.

25. Before **Apple** launched the first **iPhone** in the smartphone industry, the company designed a phone resembling the actual fruit (apple). It was a flip phone that resembled an apple when closed.

26. If you've been wondering whether it's okay or not to use your phone while charging, today you'll get your answer. Using your phone while charging reduces your battery's lifespan and eventually damages it.

Fun Time

Q. What do you hear when there is a bee on the line?
A. A buzzy signal.

27. Has your smartphone turned you into a zombie, such that you're always buried into it whenever you get the opportunity? Well, you're not alone. Studies show that 52% of teens like you are always glued to their smartphones even when they are out with friends.

 The question is, does this habit make you an inventor, does it improve your productivity, or does it just make you a consumer of data? Time is a valuable asset, the only one we have for ourselves. There is an old proverb which says "time is gold". What do you call a person who throws gold into the garbage?

 And that's not all. For example, 71% of teens love their smartphones so much; they sleep next to them now; that's the true definition of a smartphone zombie. With that in mind, know that addiction comes with tons of terrible consequences. For example, heavy smartphone usage correlates with depression.

28. It's easier to think that an electronic giant like **Samsung** began as a small electronic shop and scaled up gradually. Wrong. The company started as a grocery store in 1938 and began dealing with electronics in the 1960s.

29. You've heard of the term '**android**,' and you know it is an operating system in some smartphones. But the question is, do you know what 'android' mean? It means a human resembling a male robot.

30. When reading on your computer or smartphone, your reading speed is 10% slower than reading from a paper or a book.

31. The first text message to be sent on a cellphone was "**Merry Christmas**" on December 3, 1992. The person who sent the **SMS** was **Neil Papworth** to **Richard Jarvis**. Those days, the cell phone didn't have a keyboard, and therefore, Neil typed the message on the computer and sent it to Richard's cell phone.

32. Using your smartphone 5+ hours a day increases the chances of obesity by 43%. It is best to balance it out with exercise and to socialize face to face with others.

33. If you love your mobile phone so much that you have a great fear of losing it, you have **Nomophobia**.

Fun Time

Q. Why did the computer visit an optician?

A. It wanted to improve its websight.

34. Ever wondered who discovered the internet and how? Well, no specific person can take all the credit. That's because it took the collaboration of several engineers, scientists, and computer masters to develop a giant information center (the internet). Even so, here's a brief history of how the internet came into existence.

35. **Facebook** has over 2.79 billion monthly active users. In addition, the company owns Whatsapp, Instagram, and Facebook Messenger, with each recording over 1 billion active users. With those giant figures, these platforms have transformed the world into a tiny village. You're a message away from reaching a family member or friend globally or locally.

    Once upon a time, a scientist named **J.C.R Licklider** proposed enabling computers to communicate with each other. Other scientists advanced the idea, and in 1969, the first-ever computer communication occurred between two computers.

    But this wasn't enough.

    Those involved wanted multiple network communication and not just two. Therefore, guys buried themselves deep in research, and in the 1970s, **Robert Kahn** and V**inton Cerf** developed an internet model that allowed multiple communication networks.

    Still, it wasn't enough. Not until 1990 did a scientist, **Tim Berners-Lee**, invent the **World Wide Web** (WWW) that made the internet famous in that generation and ours today.

Fun Time

Q. What does a computer have for lunch?

A. Chips

Fun Time

How did the hippopotamus get out of the Black Sea?
A: Wet.

36. What if someone tells you that the name "Google" was discovered accidentally? Actually, it was supposed to be Googol. The mix-up occurred when the founders searched the web for "google.com" instead of "googol.com." They liked the first option and adopted it.

37. Ever wondered why the **blue** color dominates Facebook's website and mobile app? Well, the founder (Mark Zuckerberg) is red-green colorblind. That means the color he can see best is blue, and therefore, he uses it as the theme color on Facebook.

38. As a giant search engine that generates billions of revenue annually, you expect Google to mechanize all their operations - but that's not the case. For example, instead of using machines in clearing bushes, they hire a company to rent them goats to get rid of bushes and grass in their headquarters.

39. The world's first web page is still available, and you can visit it if you like. It serves as a historical archive of the **WorldWide Web**. The web page went live on the internet in 1991.Here's the link that will take you there directly http://info.cern.ch/hypertext/WWW/TheProject.html

40. Facebook is the largest social media platform, fol lowed by YouTube, WhatsApp, FB Messenger , and WeChat (consecutively)

Fun Time

Q: How many programmers does it take to fix a keyboard?
A: Zero, because it's a hardware problem.

41. Studies reveal that spending more time on social media reduces life satisfaction in all aspects except for friendships. And the effects are more adverse on girls than boys. So, if you are a heavy browser spending dozens of hours on social media daily, it may be time to reconsider.

42. Did you know that Facebook can pay you a lot of money if you find security issues in their app's program? Specifically, they are willing to pay you $500 to show them the problem in their programming method.

    This process is called **white hacking**. It refers to the process where computer experts find flaws in an application and the app owner pays them for their time and expertise, which helps them improve the efficiency of their product.

Fun Time

Q. Why should you never leave alphabet soup on your cooker while you go out?
A. Because it could spell disaster.

43. Approximately Google processes **630000** search queries per second. That is estimated at **5.6 billion** searches daily and 2 trillion yearly.

44. When you find that you can't spell a word most of the time, you are not alone because 97% of Google users type in words randomly to check whether the spelling is correct.

Fun Time

Q. What was a Pharaoh' s first words upon seeing a pyramid?
A. Look, mummy' s home.

45. There is an estimated 3.96 billion total social media users in the world. That's almost half the entire population of people on earth.

46. The first **video arcade game** existed in **1972**. The game is called **Pong**.

47. One of the largest video gaming companies, **Nintendo**, was initially established as a playing card company in **1889**. The company moved to produce toys in the 1960s. However, it wasn't until the 1970s that Nintendo ventured into video games.

48. Have you ever heard of the Ancient pyramids of **Egypt**? Well, they are among the earliest structures that prove civil engineering began far back in time. Yet, shockingly, these old pyramids still stand strong on the land of Egypt - researchers believe that they are more than 4000 years old. The age and magnificence of the pyramids attract tourists from different parts of the world. After all, who wouldn't want to see a building or structure thousands of years old?

Fun Time

Did you hear about the confused Egyptian boy?
He wondered why his daddy was a mummy.

49. **Benjamin Wright** is one of the earliest civil engineers in America, hence the title **Father of American Civil Engineering**. He played a vital role in developing America's famous canals (Artificial waterways for transportation by boats and ships) which are Ohio, Chesapeak, and Erie canals. More interestingly, you wouldn't guess the number of children Benjamin Wright had - not one, two, or five children. Instead, he had nine chi ldren, and 5 of them became engineers - they followed in their father's footsteps.

Fun Time

Tom: My dog is great at maths.
Billy: How do you know?
Tom: Yesterday, I asked her what was two minus two, and she said nothing.

50. Have you ever wondered which is the world's longest bridge? Well, even its name is very long and challenging to cram. It's called ***Danyang-Kunshan Grand Bridge***, found in China and is about 102 miles. If you're good at Maths, you've figured out already that 102 miles are equal to 164 kilometers – quite long, right?

51. **Civil Engineering** links to the 18th century (almost 200 years back), where engineers used it to describe building projects. Since then, the term "civil engineering" relates to any infrastructure project, including road, railway, bridge, and building construction.

Fun Time

Teacher: If I had four melons in one hand and five pineapples in the other, what would I have?

Pupil: Really big hands, sir

Whath is the coolest bridge you know or have ever heard of? If it isn't the **Golden Bridge** in Vietnam, you may want to think twice for the following reasons. Firstly, it is a pedestrian bridge, with the floor made of timber, but the handrails consist of stainless steel with the color of Gold.

Secondly, the curved golden bridge is held up by two giant hands made of stone - we can as well as call it "the bridge with hands." More importantly, the two huge hands are decorated with cracks and moss, giving it an ancient look of aged stone ruins. The truth is,the Golden Bridge in Vietnam is one of the coolest engineering andarchitectural structures you'll ever see.

52. Have you ever thought of a road that can link you to heaven? If so, China has got a mountain road that can almost bring your thoughts to real life. The "**heaven linking road**" climbs from the foot of **Mount Tianmen** to the top - that's a height shift from 200 meters from the ground to 1300 meters up (over 1 km high).

53. And that's not all. The road has 99 turns forming a breathtaking view of bends. An aerial view might make youthink the road is a long snake coiled many times of their product.

CHAPTER 7: ADVANCED TECHNOLOGY

Technology uses knowledge, skills, scientific processes, and methods to create new tools, gadgets, appliances, and machines. For example, humans taught themselves how to control fire, which set them apart from other animals. Today, humans create simple everyday items such as soap, paper, and sunscreen to more complex forms such as airplanes, computers, smartphones, the internet, rockets, and atomic bombs.

Fun Time

Boy: Dad, can two wrongs make a right?
Dad: No, son.
Boy: What about two Wrights? What can they do?
Dad: Make an airplane.

Another example is the rise of **robots**. Robots that can learn and make simple decisions on our behalf have been designed already.

With improved technology, tasks can be accomplished faster and more efficiently. As a result, technology has improved our lives significantly, and it helps us solve complex day-to-day problems and even have a longer life span.

Technology is moving very fast. Every year, new barriers and achievements that no one thought possible are achieved. Thanks to technology, the world as we know it today will have changed significantly in the next 20 years.

Fun Time

Teacher: Ted, as your attendance is under 50%, you will not be allowed to sit for the final exam.

Ted: No problem, sir. I am more than happy to take them standing.

Robotics

You may have heard of war robots in movies like "**Terminator**." But the truth is, such robots do exist, and the militaries worldwide have tested them. So let's explore some real-life, existing robots and find out their applications in our daily lives.

1. **Mars** is a small battle robot that the US military uses to support soldiers in wars. Until you see its capabilities on the battlefield, you can mistake it for a military toy tanker.

Surprisingly, its small frame can fit a lot of weapons ranging from non-lethal lasers that can blind enemies to machine guns for short-range shooting. As if that's not enough, the small military robot can launch tear gas and grenades....Not a toy after all, right?

The engineers of **Mars** programmed its brain to explore an area and identify dangerous spots for soldiers so that they don't have to go there and lose their lives. The best part is that the robots can make those patrols without human supervision.

Fun Time

Paul: I have a robot that is always walking into walls?
Sam: What do you call him?
Paul: Wall-E

2. **Atlas** is a robot that looks like a human with two hands and two legs. Besides, its vision is like that of a human and consists of two cameras called stereo cameras. It also has a sensor on its head that helps it sense objects on its path and avoid them.

Surprisingly, the robot can also climb and walk in the snow without help from humans. More than that, the robot has amazing gymnastic skills. It can perform handstands, somersaults, and backflips. It can also open doors, make some dance moves.

So, what are the military applications for this robot? First, the military can use Atlas to conduct dangerous search and rescue missions where humans cannot go. This can be a way of avoiding death risks in times of disaster. For example, Atlas can be sent to places with high levels of radioactivity that can be dangerous to human beings. They can also be sent to unstable buildings and war zones where bullets are being exchanged every second. This way, robots help to preserve human life.

Fun Time

Q: What' s the robot' s favorite chair?
A: Electric-chair

2. **About** is a police robot developed by the National Defence University in China. The developers designed it to independently patrol the streets for up to 8 hours and protect people against violence. In fact, it can move at a maximum speed of 18 km/hrs to rush over to a scene or chase down fleeing criminals.

This robot can chase down criminals. It has a secret weapon on the criminals -- a mild electric shock that is not dangerous.

And even better, Anbot can recharge itself without human intervention. That's cool, right? In general, Anbot can be an added security measure to enhance human police patrol.

Have you ever imagined yourself with a robot pet? If so, some technology researchers claim that 2025 might be the year of pet bots. But how true is that? The chance is that they are mostly right, especially if you consider that some people in Japan already have robot dogs as pets and not toys. It's true. The robot dogs (known as Aibos) come from Sony and are primarily for company and comfort.

Fun Time

Q: What do you say when a robot dies?
A: Rust in peace.

This robot can chase down criminals. It has a secret weapon on the criminals -- a mild electric shock that is not dangerous.

And even better, Anbot can recharge itself without human intervention. That's cool, right? In general, Anbot can be an added security measure to enhance human police patrol.

Have you ever imagined yourself with a robot pet? If so, some technology researchers claim that 2025 might be the year of pet bots. But how true is that? The chance is that they are mostly right, especially if you consider that some people in Japan already have robot dogs as pets and not toys. It's true. The robot dogs (known as Aibos) come from Sony and are primarily for company and comfort.

Fun Time

Robot 1: Humans make me so angry.
Robot 2: Why?
Robot 1: They are always pushing my buttons.

Now that you've heard a lot about automated robots let's see what it takes to become a robot expert. The simplest definition of a robot would be a man-made imitation of humans and animals. Thus, they are machines that are designed to copy human behavior.

So, what's the difference between robots and other types of machines such as cars? If you want to understand the engineering concept behind the electronic and mechanical parts that make up a robot, then the field of science called **Mechatronics** would be perfect for you.

For the robot's brain, you can study programming and computer engineering to program the robot or, at a higher level, use artificial intelligence (we will cover in the next section) to automate the robot's decision-making. But after becoming an expert in all of those, what are the possible jobs you can follow in your life? Well, as in the future, everything will become as automated as possible, and robots can work 24/7. So being a robotic engineer is a good secure job.

Well, you'll have to master something called **Robotic Process Automation (RPA)**. With these skills, you can secure the following giant-pay jobs:

- Robotic Process Automation Analyst
- Robotic Process Automation Architect
- Robotic Process Automation Developer

Fun Time

Q. What do robots also order when they eat salsa?
A. Micro-chips

Making robots is not hard; you can make your robot. The brain system is the main part of a robot. It controls all the other parts of the robot. For that, you can use a small piece of hardware known as Raspberry Pi. With **Raspberry Pi**, you can create and program your robot (if you buy the robotic kit) You can even create your owngame using this new technological equipment

The first thing you will need is a **keyboard**. With the keyboard, youcan connect the Raspberry Pi so that you can program and monitorit. You can even connect it to the TV to see your codes. Yourrobot's brain will be ready as soon as you are done with theprogramming. Put the robot brain in the robot's kit and watch itoperate. Then, you can show it to your friends and enjoy operatingit together.

Fun Time

Q. What did the robot use to cross the river?
A. A ro-boat.

Artificial Intelligence & Machine Learning

Humans have always enjoyed inventing and creating new things. Most of the time, inventions are driven by need. They make life easier. Human beings' ultimate goal and dream have always been to invent something that can think and learn like us.

Some people argue that it makes us feel like a god, for example. We are far from that, but we have made significant progress in that direction in fields such as **Machine Learning (ML) and Artificial Intelligence (AI).**

With AI and ML technology, robots and machines can solve problems the same way human beings do. The application of AI is a lot, considering that wherever you need to make decisions, an AI model can be trained to make the same decision if that decision is repetitive. An example is, stopping at a red light or answering greetings or doing math, or detecting if an egg has a crack on it or not. Thus, we can train machines to do the same decision-making we do as humans.

Fun Time

Q. What plant do baby chicks like the best

A. EGG-plants

A **smartphone** can detect and recognize you. It can also unlock the phone for you, depending on the settings. It can also detect objects such as animals and fruits when a photograph is being taken.

Tesla has developed electric cars that can detect other cars, human beings, and even traffic lights.

Fun Time

Q. Have you ever seen an egg laugh?
A. If you did, you would notice it cracks up.

Another good example is the video suggestions YouTube gives you when you watch some specific videos. The computer has been trained to select videos similar to yours depending on what you searched for or the videos you liked, or what other kids around your age are interested in.

Netflix also similarly gives suggestions.
Google maps also generate voices that sound like humans to give you directions and guide you whenever you need to turn as you are driving.

All these are examples of AI and MI in use.

Fun Time

How to watch a movie nowadays:

1. Going to Netflix.
2. Check 100 films tutorials.
3. Landing on a TV series.
4. Finally ending in watching the episodes you liked before.

For example, AI can help us make better and more accurate decisions. How? Scientists simulate how the human brain works. The answer is by replicating the neurons, which are the building blocks of the brain. How? They use mathematics and statistics to imitate how a single neuron reacts when it receives signals from other neurons and sensors in our body.

The scientists then implement that mathematical model using computer programs. This makes it possible for that model to be run by computers. The computers can do exactly as they are told.

Fun Time

Q. Which part of math do kids who wear glasses enjoy the most?
A. Di-vision

Different computer languages are used to instruct computers to perform specific tasks; languages like **Python, C++, Java, R,** and **Assembly**. The specific language chosen depends on the task the computer is required to do. For example, some languages are faster, like C++, while others can easily write and implement complicated scientific notions like Python.

Fun Time

A programmer once said, What I coded at the beginning is only me and god could understand it.

But now, after a month of checking it out, only God knows.

Still, others are very flexible and provide programmers with tools called libraries which they can use whenever they want to implement complicated mathematical ideas like the R language.

Human beings can learn and generalize their knowledge. So scientists tried to mathematically replicate how the lowest element of human brains (neurons) and human brains operate. Using mathematical statistics, they instruct a system called the neural network.

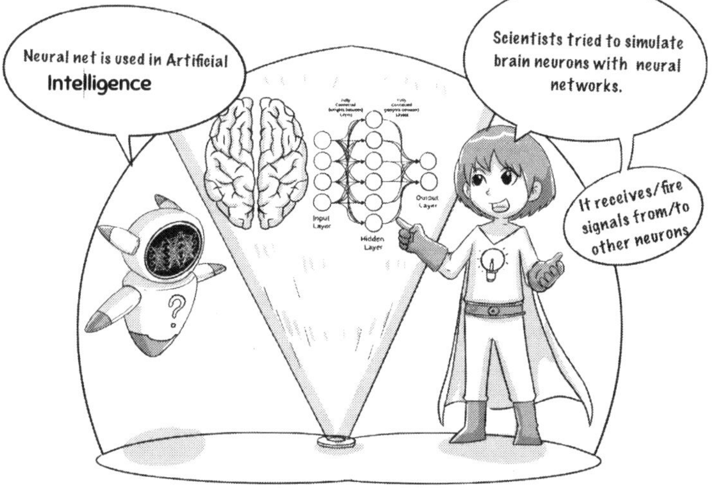

This technology also enables robots and machines to learn from statistics and remember patterns as they are supposed to be used, improving order and safety.

One good example is the **smartphone personal assistant** (like google assistant for android devices) that answers users' questions instantly and helps in device management. Like **Siri** on Apple phones and pc, **Cortona** on windows, **Alexa** from Amazon. You have been taking advantage of AI during the day when you see a suggestion from youtube or new suggestions on Facebook/ Instagram.

Fun Time

Q. If an Apple user stares you in the eye, what would you describe it as?
A. iContact

Fun Time

Q: What does it say on Steve Jobs' gravestone?
A: I am Steve Jobs, I am creative, and I created the iPod, iMac, iPad, iTunes, iCloud, iPhone, iRIP

Here are some interesting career paths you can follow if you are interested in Artificial Intelligence:

- Artificial Intelligence Research Scientist
- Artificial Intelligence Architect
- Artificial Intelligence Engineer
- Machine Learning Engineer

Fun Time

Girl: In what way are data like people?
Boy: Sorry, I do not know.
Girl: If you interrogate it hard enough, it will tell you exactly what you want to know

Computer Vision

Imagine that you have a robot, and you want it to see the world the way you do. You also want it to make decisions the way you would when you see the world around you. For example, you want it to move in the house without hitting walls and chairs. Or you want the robot to look at you when you are talking to it or be able to fetch you your cup of coffee from the kitchen. Computer vision can help you teach the robot how to detect different objects in the room like the walls, the coffee cup, or your face.

This field is very popular in the industrial world because there are thousands of tasks that need human supervision, for example, monitoring a production line or even checking if a product is not defective. Using smart surveillance cameras, they can automatically spot some suspicious behavior and then alert an agent, like detecting someone walking at night in your backyard, using infrared cameras.

Fun Time

Man 1: I am so pleased I do not have 20/20 vision.
Man 2: Why?
Man 1: Because I have no desire to ever see 2020 again (because of covid).

Fun Time

Q. What did the doctor say to the camera that was depressed and had mood swings?

A. I think you have a bipolaroid disorder.

Computer vision is also used in the medical field. For example, it can detect **Alzheimer's Disease** by taking pictures of the people's retina in their eyes or detecting tumors using **MRI images**.

On top of that, computer vision comes with a wide application. For starters, some smartphone features like Apple's **FaceID** uses face recognition to control phone access. Another application is gaming. For example, Microsoft used **Kinect** to detect human body parts and apply their reactions in games or other applications.

Also, **computer vision** plays an essential role in security/traffic cameras, and most importantly, it's the whole idea in creating driverless cars and most robots. Think about it. Can driverless cars operate if they can't see where they are going?......... Of course not. That will be like having a blind driver in control of the car. Therefore, computer vision plays a critical role in such sectors of technology.

Fun Time

Q. Where would dogs go when they need to park their cars?
A. To a barking lot.

Virtual Reality

Virtual Reality is commonly referred to as **VR**. It is a computer technology that makes you feel like you are in a different location from the real one. The images, sounds, and physical sensations are created using different kinds of software. The new location can be another country which you can tour or an exciting game that you can play.

For example, imagine yourself sitting in your room on your chair. Then you put on a magical glass, and you suddenly find yourself in a whole new world in front of a pirate ship. But it's not limited to that, and it's not like a static movie on TV or cinema. It's as real as it can get. When you turn your head to the right, you see two pirates cleaning their guns, and on your left, a captain is looking through his monocular.

Fun Time

Q. What TV station does Christopher Columbus watch every day?
A. The Discovery Channel

You can actually look up and down the ship, walk on the ship, go down the deck and explore around. Well, this technology is called **VR** or **Virtual Reality**. But it doesn't end here. With this technology, you can interact with the environment by some probes and shoot the guns in the game. The screen changes based on your head orientation and moves in that direction.

VR facts every kid should know:

1. One specific person did not invent virtual reality. Many people contributed to the growth of technology. There are at least five people who can claim ownership of Virtual Reality.

2. Did you know that virtual reality is being used in healthcare too? It's not just about fun and games. Virtual reality is helping medics to treat people with **depression**, Post Traumatic Stress Disorder (PTSD), and **anxiety**.

3. In 2015, **Marriot** announced that it could transport people from London to Mau in less than 2 minutes. Virtual Reality Travel is super-real.

4. Morton Heilig created the first VR headset, and he named it "**Telesphere Mask**".

5. Approximately **171 million people** today use Virtual Reality.

6. **79% of people** who try Virtual Reality fall in love with it and try it again. **52% of consumers** want to be associated with brands that support Virtual Reality.

7. **96% of consumers** between the ages of 14-19 said they are interested in Virtual Reality.

8. By 2025, an **estimated 500 million** Virtual Reality headsets will be sold.

9. **80% of people** who try Virtual Reality inform their friends about it.

10. Did you know that by 2023 the Virtual Reality market will reach approximately $34 billion? Combined with **Augmented Reality**, the total is estimated at $94 billion.

Fun Time

Kid: Mum says she will give $20 if I promise to be good.
Dad: You' re lucky. When I was your age, people were trading with chocolates, I suppose.

Augmented Reality

Do you think Virtual Reality is cool? Well, Augmented Reality is more exciting and practical than VR. An example of Augmented Reality is used on Snapchats and Apple phones. When you want to take pictures, and you add digital glasses on your face or add dog ears to your picture, that's Augmented Reality.

The glasses and the dog ears are not on your face, but you see them on the picture on your phone. That's where the augmentedword comes from, and it adds more to your current reality—the cool applications of Augmented Reality range from gaming to industryand personal daily usage.

Le'ts say for example that your dad is in a store looking to buy a new couch. However, he is unsure about how any of the couches will look in the living room. He would be able to visualize how the couches could look in the room with AR.

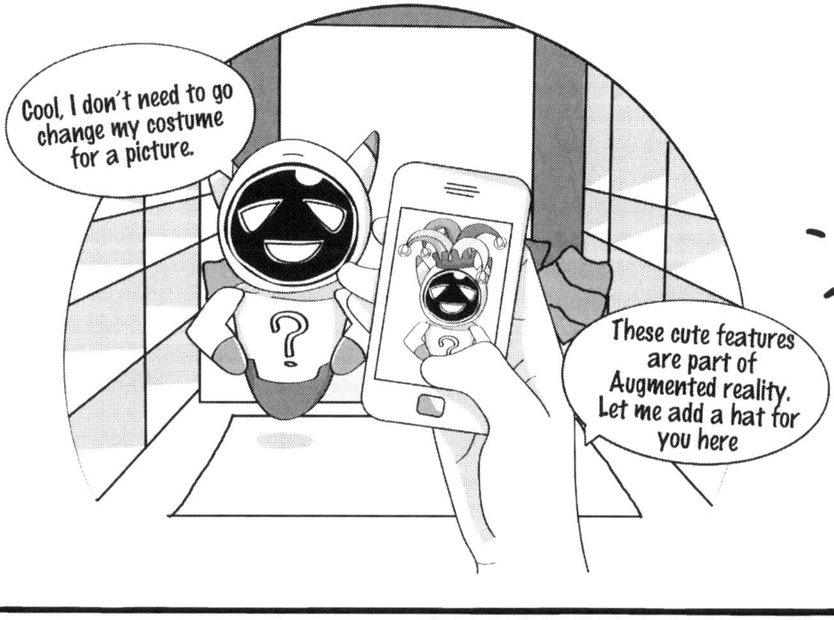

Fun Time

Q. What did the boy say after taking a video of his shoe?
A. I was pleased with that footage.

5G Network

The good news is that all of the above is possible. That's because super strong internet connectivity, called 5G, is about to take over from the present famous 4G. What's cool about the 5G network is that its speed is up to 10-20 times faster than 4G. That is to say, if it takes you 10 minutes (in a 4G network) to download a 1 GB file, then you'll only need a minute to download the same file (in a 5G network). That's pretty fast.

But is 5G only beneficial when streaming videos or playing online games? Let's find out.

5G will improve the way data is collected from machines, driverless cars, and robots. It will also improve how different devices communicate and how they are managed from one place. One good example of device-to-device communication is vehicle-to-vehicle communication for safety. For example, if a car in front breaks suddenly, the vehicles behind would get a signal and stop immediately before an accident happens.

Fun Time

Q. Do you know why traffic lights are always turning red?
A. It is probably because they have to change in front of everyone who is watching them?

Cloud Computing

Imagine you have a notebook, and if you put it on your bookshelf at home, you don't need to bring it anywhere. You can have access to it in school, at your friend's house, in your grandparents' house on the bus or in another country. This is possible for your notebook's digital version and any other digital form of data like images, songs, and videos.

Cloud computing is the process of providing computing services such as storage and knowledge through the internet.

For example, instead of saving your favorite movies, music videos, games, and pictures on your computer, you can save them online, somewhere on the internet (a cloud). This way, you can share, watch and edit them anytime you like.

Fun Time

I stopped connecting my phone to the cloud.
Why?
I kept getting missed calls.

If you lose your computer or even drop your phone in water,you can easily access your movies, games, pictures, and musicvideos using another phone or computer because they are storedon the internet and not the computer. Instead of relying on yourcomputer storage, like it was done traditionally, you can takeadvantage of the help from internet storage. This is a singleexample of cloud computing.

Think about big companies like Google, Youtube, or Banks. Theyhave a lot of data to work with and store. If their computers fail,maybe due to malicious attacks from cybercriminals, they couldsuffer huge losses of data. Fortunately, they can store all the dataon "the cloud" on the internet and access it whenever they can.Even if their computers crash, their data is still safe.

Imagine you have a notebook, and if you put it on your bookshelf at home, you don't need to bring it anywhere. You can have access to it in school, at your friend's house, in your grandparents' house on the bus or in another country. This is possible for your notebook's digital version and any other digital form of data like images, songs, and videos.

Cloud computing is the process of providing computing services such as storage and knowledge through the internet.

For example, instead of saving your favorite movies, music videos, games, and pictures on your computer, you can save them online, somewhere on the internet (a cloud). This way, you can share, watch and edit them anytime you like.

Fun Time

Q. Why is the Apple computing system the only choice in space?
A. Because it is not possible to open windows.

Note that cloud computing is not only for storing data. After storage, it comes to processing the data. Now imagine that you have a computer and you have a game on it, consider that you can play that game with your friends at the same time (on your computer) 1, 2, 3 friends could work but when it comes to 1000 players, at some point your computer will crash because it doesn't have enough resources to run that game smoothly for everyone.

That's the same thing that happens with big companies like banks, **Netflix** (movie sharing), **Spotify** (music sharing), **Airbnb** (house-sharing), **Air Canada** (airlines), or any company that has thousands of clients. As a result, these companies must increase their resources rapidly when they have more clients. Which is called scaling, and cloud computing allows that to happen. That's why you can access lots of services online rapidly and seamlessly.

Most companies such as Airbnb, Amazon, banks, and government agencies are now using cloud computing to protect their data if their computers break down or their hard drives fail.

Fun Time

Winnie: I hate my new job. I have to sit on a computer for at least 10 hours a day.

Barry: I am sure that is not good for your computer. I recommend you sit on a chair instead.

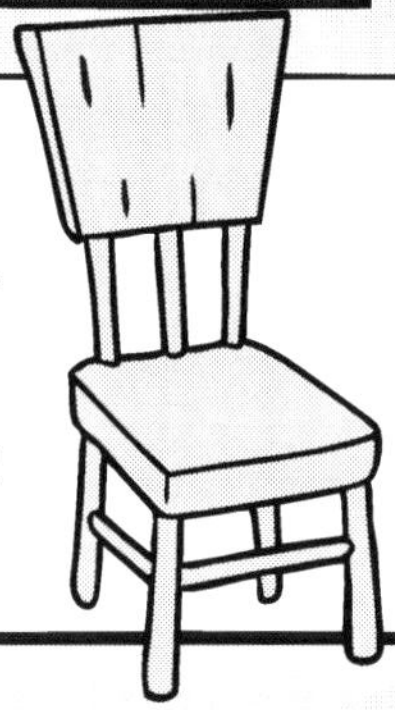

Quantum Computing

When humans invent something, they always want to make it faster, stronger, bigger, and easier to work with. So, just like cars, houses, buildings, phones, TVs, and computers, human beings are always looking for ways to make them better.

Imagine you have a computer that is so fast it can try all combinations of the passwords anyone has on their computers and crack it in a second. Then you would be the king; you can solve some of the most complicated problems with billions of combinations. You can win a game of chess against a chessmasters, find the best formulas for specific medicines, and cure diseases. You can predict complicated patterns in the **stockmarket** and build a large amount of wealth.

For this reason, researchers have developed next-level computers called quantum computers. The new computer models are believed to operate at a mind-blowing speed and solve many complex problems at once, unlike the supercomputers you know. And when you hear "mind-blowing," it's a speed you can't begin to imagine.
Why?

Here's the answer. You'll need experience with:

- Quantum Mechanics
- Linear Algebra
- Probability
- Machine Learning
- Information Technology

Fun Time

Boy: Mom, why do you think computers are so smart?
Mom: I guess it is because they are willing to listen to their motherboards.

Cybersecurity

Consider that you want to keep away the thieves from your home. What would you do?

Well, you could build a wall or a fence around your place, or add a camera or change your house lock to something more advanced and hard to open with just a wire.

The same solution applies to virtual environments like the internet:

If you want to keep your computer and files on your system away from **hackers(thieves)**, you can apply several techniques known as cybersecurity.

Fun Time

Man 1: If I was a hacker, I would use hydroponics to grow plants.
Man 2: Why is that?
Man: Then I would get root access.

Hacker Types:

- **Ethical Hackers** – who offer help to internet users like troubleshooting risks on websites and internet accounts.

- **Malicious Hackers** – They steal information for their gains or destroy other people's data. But what exactly do hackers do? Why do internet users fear them so much?

Malicious hackers are webmasters highly skilled in computing processes like coding or programming. However, instead of using these skills well, they use them to exploit vulnerable websites and computers by stealing sensitive information like passwords to bank or premium accounts on the internet.

Fun Time

Q: What' re the most unpleasant two steps in a hacker' s pathway?
A: two-step verification, of course.

To do all these terrible things, such hackers create harmful programs called malware. They then trick their targets using cunning tricks to accept the malware, and then they exploit them without mercy.

Malware has different names; one of them is Trojan Horses. Its naming is based on ancient Greek stories of the siege of Troy. Greeks couldn't infiltrate Troy's tall walls, so they decided to pretend like they had abandoned the siege and left only one big wooden horse as a symbol of their defeat. The people of Troy were so happy that they took the wooden horse in the city and began to celebrate around it.

Fun Time

Girl: Mom, where is daddy taking my sick pony?
Mom: To the hospital

When the city of **Troy** went to sleep, Greek soldiers that were hidden inside the wooden horse got out secretly and opened the gates of Troy, and the city Fell. **Trojan horses'** malware work the same way. They look like good software you download on your computer, but they open some ports on your system and facilitate hackers to access your computer.

For this reason, **cybersecurity** remains a major trend in technology because internet security measures must constantly evolve to defend against malicious hackers.

And to prove that this is true, big platforms like **Google** and **Facebook** are willing to pay good money to anyone who can identify **security vulnerabilities** in their programs. That rests the case: Cybersecurity must go hand in hand with advancing technology because malicious hackers are here to stay.

If you want to fight against malicious hackers when you grow up, the following are some job opportunities you'll get:

- Ethical Hacker
- Security Engineer
- Malware Analyst
- Chief Security Officer

Most Technologically Advanced Countries

Did you know that countries in Asia dominate the world of technology? South Korea, Singapore, Japan, and China are amongst the world's leading tech-forward countries. Other countries well advanced in technology include Germany, the USA, Switzerland, Israel, France, Sweden, Denmark, and Finland.

Fun Time

Officer: Sailor, how did that hacker manage to escape?
Sailor: I guess he used the backdoor and some ransomware, sir.

Advanced technological expertise is one of the most important things a country can possess. Unfortunately, the demand for technological skills is higher than the supply. But people in countries leading the pack enjoy the best healthcare, reliable transportation, the biggest and best industries, and high manufacturing potential, and excellent schooling systems.

Germany is home to Volkswagen, a motor vehicle manufacturer, Siemens, a huge company that deals with transport, healthcare, infrastructure, and technology. Not only is Germany a highly-respected engineering company, but it also has some of the best schools, universities, military technology, infrastructure, and medicine.

South Korea is home to big companies such as Samsung, LG, and Hyundai.
In Singapore, the productivity and expertise of citizens rise every day. 89% of its citizens pursue higher education, according to a study done in 2018.

Now, think of Google, Microsoft, Apple, and Facebook, and you have some of the most powerful and influential companies in the world. They are all American-based companies. The US has very powerful technology. The US is also a leader in telecommunication, space technology, military, and pharmaceuticals.

Fun Time

Q. Where do you go in Germany to have good pork for breakfast?
A. Ham-burg

The Biggest Technology Giants in the World

The most powerful technology companies in the world generate a lot of money. As a result, such companies thrive even in the middle of a pandemic or an economic crisis.

You might be familiar with most of them because they are very famous and quite popular. Apple, Microsoft, Google are the biggest technologically advanced companies in the world. Other big shots include **Instagram**, **Linked In**, and **Adobe**. **Microsoft** owns **LinkedIn**, and **Facebook** owns **Instagram**.

The **US** dominates the world of technology. It is home to 14 of the most powerful tech companies. It is closely followed by **China** which is home to **Tencent**, a social media and entertainment company.

The universities and organizations that contribute widely to research include:

- Chinese Academy of Sciences
- Harvard University
- Stanford University
- Max Planck Society
- National Centre for Scientific Research
- Massachusetts Institute of Technology
- The University of Cambridge
- Peking University
- Helmholtz Association of German Research Centres
- The University of Tokyo

Fun Time

Q: What is the magic formula to having the most popular Facebook profile?A: ctrl+C (copy) and ctrl+V (paste)

Nanotech

Imagine yourself climbing off your bed only to find out that youhave shrunk by about 2000 times. If you walked to your living room, you would come across shrunken chairs, computers, tablets, andpeople. The only problem is that these things would be so smallthat you would only see the cells and molecules they are made of.Nevertheless, you would be able to move the items around and playaround with them.

Now, assume that you decided to stick these molecules togetheragain in interesting ways. You would start building fancy things such asmedicine, cars, houses, and even computers. Well, this is whatexperts refer to as **nanotechnology**.

It is the process and art of building things using a very small scalecalled "nanoscale." Nanotechnology is a fast-growing branch ofscience and technology. Nanotechnology can be used to createsmall machines such as engines, pumps, gears, and even switchest hat are very easy to operate.

They can be used to create tiny robots that are sent to hazardousareas to clean nuclear plants. They are called nanobots and fallunder the nanorobotic domain.

Fun Time

Maggie: Listen, Penny, can you hear that computer squeaking?
Penny: Yes. Maybe someone has stepped on its mouse.

You could be wearing nanotechnology pants as you are reading this. Nanotechnology clothes are made from fibers whose surfaces areso small that dirt particles cannot penetrate them. This means thatthe material will stay clean for a long time.

Cosmetic companies also use anotechnology to create certain brands of sunscreen. The sunscreen creates a microscopiclayer on the skin that harmful sun rays cannot penetrate.

Fun Time

Q. Why did the computer feel cold?
A. It had left the windows open.

CHAPTER 8: FAMOUS THEORIES, PHILOSOPHERS, AND SCIENTISTS

The human race has studied the world for thousands of years. And several curious people began to explore and question whatever they saw around them. They went on to make discoveries. For example, Christopher Columbus went on to discover America by choosing to go in a different direction. Isaac Newton discovered gravity after becoming curious about why an apple falls to the ground instead of going up.

Many of these inventors created products and devices that have revolutionized all areas of our lives. These discoveries have influenced how we live our lives and have given us answers to questions we never thought we could understand.

Let's explore some famous scientists, philosophers, and their famous discoveries. But first,

What is a Nobel Prize?

Nobel Prizes are a group of honors awarded to scientists who contribute the best works in economics, sciences (physics,chemistry, mathematics, biology) literature, and medicine. It is the highest academic honor in the world.

Alfred Nobel was a peace advocate during his lifetime. When he died, he asked that the money in his will be used to award peace advocates like him. Thus, in 1901, the honorary awards called Nobel Prizes, named after Alfred Nobel, were invented.

Fun Time

Q. How was Gregor Mendel honored for his achievements in the field of genetics?

A. He was awarded the Nobel Peas Prize.

What does it take to win a Nobel Prize?

Well, there is no one specific formula used to choose a Nobel Prize winner. Instead, there are common characteristics that can be found in the winners. These characteristics can help us to understand what it takes to win. For example, most winners have come up with solutions to difficult problems. Their solutions have helped human beings and even saved many lives—for example, vaccines and drugs.

Other winners have improved our knowledge of certain subjects such as Chemistry, Maths, Biology, Environment, and Physics.

Alexander Fleming won the Nobel Prize for discovering Penicillin, a drug used to treat many diseases such as meningitis, pneumonia, and scarlet fever.

Albert Einstein was awarded the Nobel Prize for his contribution to Physics, and **Robert Koch** got one for discovering bacteria. Most recently, **Ralph Steinman** won the award for his contribution to cancer vaccines research.

Leaders who fight for the preservation of peace are also likely to win the Nobel Prize. For example, **Martin Luther King Jr.** was a civil rights leader and an activist. He won the Nobel Prize for his contribution to world peace.

Most recently, **Ralph Steinman** won the awardfor his contribution to cancer vaccines research.

Esther Duflo is a French-American economistwho won the Nobel prize with her team for their experimental research to decrease global poverty.

Olga Tokarczuk, is a Polish writer and also an activist. She won the Nobel Prize in Literature forher style of writing that represents crossing the boundaries as a form of life.

Fun Time

Q. What can we say about Nobel prize winners and farmers?
A. They are both performing well in their fields.

Michael Faraday: Father of Electricity

What would life be without electricity? No Tv, no phones, no video games, or even ice cream!

Michael Faraday was born in 1791 into a very poor family. Being the son of a simple London blacksmith, Faraday only received a basic education. However, when he was 14, he got a job as a bookbinder's assistant. He worked there for seven years, and during this time, he read many science books and taught himself a lot of scientific principles.

In 1821, he came up with one of the most important inventions in history—the electric motor and made his first transformer. He published his discoveries about electromagnetic rotation and electromagnetic induction, the concepts behind generators and transformers.

His discoveries made it possible for electricity to be transformed into a powerful invention. Faraday found a way to convert magnetic force into electric force using electromagnetic induction.

Electricity was first used to power the light in a British lighthouse. Many also refer to him as the **Father of Electromagnetism**. Even to this day, his name is honored as a unit of measurement. The "**Farad**" is used to describe electric capacity (electrical capacitance).

Michael Faraday also made other important discoveries, and his ideas have been used to develop other inventions such as the telegraph. Look around you, and you will not miss something Faraday's lifelong work contributed to.

Fun Time

There were three photos of famous scientists on Albert Einstein's desk. He used them for inspiration. It is interesting to note that one of these pictures was that of Michael Faraday.

Lawrence Roberts

Lawrence used the technique to transfer the information between two computers and connect them. His workers ended up developing the internet, and in 2001 he won the Draper Prize for that.

Tim Berners Lee: Invented the World Wide Web

Imagine a world without the **World Wide Web**. You would never be able to access the internet. A computer scientist and engineer known as **Tim Berners-Lee** has been widely credited with the invention of the worldwide web that enables us to access the internet. His first theories for such a system were described in a 1989 proposal, but it wasn't until 1991 that the world's first website was published online.

Fun Time

Spider 1: Can I borrow your computer?
Spider 2: Of course. Why do you need it?
Spider 1: I need to check my website.

His first invention of the world wide web had the first web browser, hyper texting, and Berner-Lee.

Thanks to **Tim Berners Lee**, you can watch educational YouTube videos, attend online classes and meetings, you can post on TikTok, Instagram, Facebook, or Snapchat, and even send emails and texts to your friends very fast.

Fun Time

Q. When does a website fail at a tennis game?
A. When its server not available.

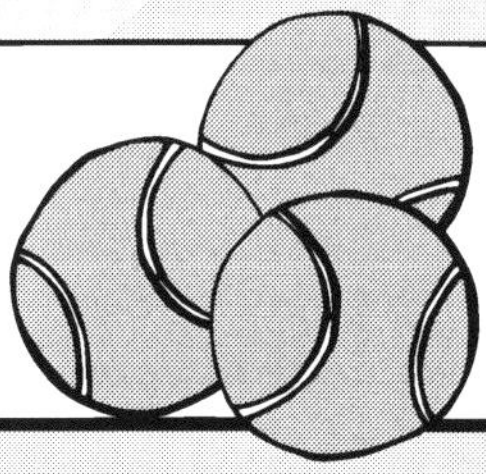

Marie Sklodowska Curie: Discovered Radioactivity & Elements

Did you know that **Marie Curie** was the first woman to win a Nobel Prize? What did the photochemist say to the radiation physicist? Can you shed some light on this matter? Did you know she remainsthe only person to ever win Nobel prizes for two separate branches of science?

Fun Time

Q. What kind of humor do primary elements prefer?
A. Well, Sulfur, Argon, Calcium, and Samarium, which is called SArCaSm

As Marie Curie studied the element called **Uranium**, she realized that it gave off rays, which she named "**radioactivity**." She went on todiscover two very powerful elements in the periodic table; Radiumand Polonium.

Well, Marie was a very smart woman. In 1903, she received her firstNobel Prize in Physics and two other people, one of whom was herhusband, for her amazing discoveries. In 1911, she won the same award in Chemistry, which cemented her legacy in science.

She was a pioneer in the modern-day medical use of radioactivity.She even trained nurses in radiography (using x-rays to take picturesof body images) in World War II and helped save many lives.

Sadly, the frequent exposure to high amounts of radiation made hersick, and she died of cancer later on in 1934.

Fun Time

Q. What does Marie Curie eat when she goes out?
A. Fission chips

Wilhelm Roentgen: Discovered X-rays

Did you know that Rontgen was the very first Nobel Prize winner in Physics? He received this award in 1901 while working as a professorat the **University of Wurzburg**, Germany. The first **X-ray** ever taken was that of his wife's hand.

Fun Time

Marie: Do you think dogs can read x-rays and MRIs?
Bill: I doubt it, but catscan (CT scan is also known as CATSCAN)

Not long after he discovered X-rays, he also invented X-ray photography Rontgen's university soon discovered that the invention would transform and help in the diagnosis and treatment of many diseases and bone injuries, and it awarded him a direct honorary degree in medicine. The discovery of X-rays was one of the most important discoveries in medicine, not to mention molecular and atomic science.

Alexander Graham Bell: Invented the Telephone

What would life be without a **telephone**? We would never have modern-day smartphones. It would be impossible to communicate with your friends, parents, or even siblings. It would take days to send and receive messages using letters sent at the post office.

Fun Time

Martin: Sally, can you think of a word that starts with e, ends with e, but only has one letter.

Sally: Does such a word exist?
Martin: Yes, envelope

Alexander Graham Bell was a naturally curious and intelligent person. He created a simple receiver that could transform electricity into sound. With this discovery, he invented the telephone in 1876 when he was only 29 years old. In 1876, he was given an exclusive right to ownership for his invention.

He later formed the **Bell Telephone Company** in the same year and gained enormous financial and technical success.

Fun Time

Q. What song would there be if you put a skunk and a bell together?
A. Jingle smells

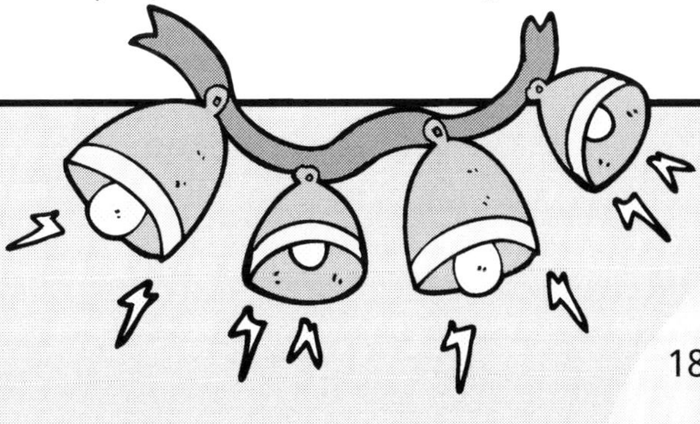

Alexander Bell was awarded the **French Volta Price** in 1880, and he used the money to create the **Volta Laboratory** in Washington. He continued to do medical research and experiments in communication until he died in 1922.

Fun Time

Q. What gets a lot of answers even though it never asks any Questions?
A. A telephone.

Fun Facts About Alexander Graham Bell

1. During his burial, all telephone services in America were stopped for a single minute to honor him.

2. In 1877, Connecticut became the first place in the world with a telephone exchange system.

3. His middle name was a birthday present. He was named Alexander Bell at birth, and he wished he could have a middle name. His father and grandfather were both named Alexander Bell. Many people believe he wanted to differentiate himself from both of them. On his 11th birthday, his father let him adopt Graham as his middle name.

4. He invented the wireless telephone. He created a telephone which transmitted conversations using light beams called photophones.

5. He faced over 600 lawsuits over his invention of the telephone. Many people claimed that they had invented the telephone too, and they took him to court. Five of the lawsuits filed against him reached the Supreme court, but his patent was always upheld.

Louis Pasteur: Discovered Pasteurization

Have you ever wondered where maggots found in food such as meat and fruits come from? Louis Pasteur, a French **microbiologist** and chemist, discovered that **microorganisms** in food cause **fermentation** and can also cause diseases in human beings. In simpler terms, he discovered that germs caused illnesses, and they also made food go bad.

Fun Time

Doctor: I looked at your X-ray and found a broken rib?
Patient: That sounds bad.
Doctor: Don't worry. I fixed it with Photoshop.

If germs were responsible for destroying food, then heating the food to certain temperatures to kill the germs could stop the food from getting spoilt without the taste being affected. For example, France's economy was widely dependent on wine, but it went bad frequently. If the wine could be heated to 55 degrees Celsius, the bacteria could be destroyed, and the wine would stay fresh for long without losing its original taste.

This process is known as **pasteurization**, in honor of his name, **Pasteur**. It is still widely used today to extend the shelf life of both packaged and non-packaged foods such as milk, certain beverages, and fruit juice.

He was also passionate about finding treatment and cures for diseases. In the process, he discovered that vaccines could prevent diseases. He created vaccines for dangerous, life-threatening diseases such as cholera, rabies, and anthrax. He pioneered research on the concept of immunity and immunology and prepared a path for others to follow.

Fun Time

Q. If you were in a cold room, what would you do to keep warm?
A. Go and stand in a corner. It is probably 90 degrees there.

George Washington Carver: Plant Doctor

Did you know that George Washington Carver made more than 300 products (including gasoline, dyes, and plastics) from peanuts alone? He was known as "Peanut Man" because of his wide knowledge and understanding of the legume and its use (he didn't invent the peanut butter, though).

Fun Time

Did you know George Washington always had problems getting to sleep?He said it was because he couldn't lie.

George Washington was an African-American scientist who was born into slavery in 1860. He struggled to get an education, but he eventually graduated with a degree in Agriculture in 1894, against all odds. He made great contributions to agricultural chemistry.

He introduced the idea of crop rotation to poor farmers in rural areas. Carver experimented with sweet potatoes, cotton, peanut butter, and many other crops. His goal was to help farmers improve the nutritional value of their diets. As a result, many people see him as the savior of the agricultural economy in the rural south.

Fun Time

George Washington Carver's monument as a boy was the first national memorial ever done for an African American.

Ibn al-Haytham: Optics (How the Eyes Work)

Ibn al-Haytham was an Arab physicist, mathematician, and astronomer. He experimented widely on light and in **optics** (which is how the eyes work). He correctly discovered that we can only see objects when light enters our eyes and not because our eyes emit light (this is how ancient Greek philosophers argued).

Fun Time

Q. What do teachers and optometrists have in common?
A. It is both their jobs to test pupils.

He studied the structure of the eyes and how they work using a bull's eye. He also proved that light travels in straight lnes. Before Isaac Newton's discoveries, Ibn al-Haytham's Book of Optics was the most important book on the subject.

Alexander Fleming: Discovered Penicillin

On August 6th, 1881, **Alexander Fleming**, a Scottish scientist, famously known for discovering **Penicillin** in 1928. He came home from a two-week vacation to discover that some molds had accidentally contaminated a staphylococcus culture plate and that the mold prevented the growth of the disease-causing bacteria known as staphylococci. For this reason, Alexander Fleming saw his accomplishment as accidental. He believed that because he didn't plan them, he saw it as something that happened by chance.

Fun Time

Q. What would you always see with antibiotics?
A. Unclebiotics.

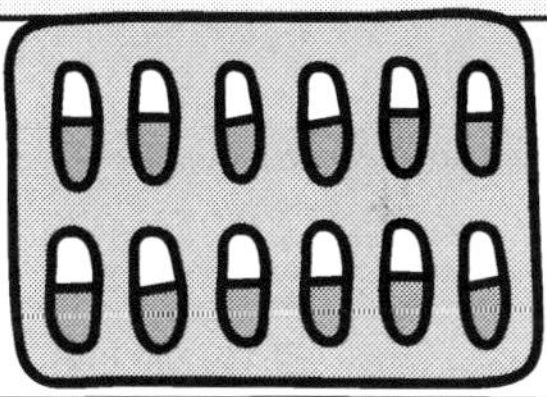

Penicillin was a revolutionary antibiotic. It was the world's first bacterial killer. In 1945, he received a Nobel Prize for Physiology and Medicine for his discovery.

Ernst Chain and **Howard Flory** from the University of Oxford continued research and finished Fleming's discoveries after studying Penicillin in 1931. Penicillin has saved millions of lives by enabling physicians to cure life-threatening diseases such as meningitis, syphilis, pneumococcal pneumonia, gonorrhea, among many others.

Even better is that Penicillin greatly reduced the death and amputation of troops in World War II. Records show that only 400 million units of Penicillin had been manufactured in the early months of 1943, but America was producing up to 650 billion units per month by the time World War II ended in 1945.

Fun Time

Q. Why do bacteria always come last in math exams?
A. Because they multiply by dividing

Zhang Heng

Born in 78 CE, **Zhang Heng** was an intelligent inventor and astronomer from China. He discovered the very complex scientific concept of the moon not being a light source. He correctly argued that the moon reflected light from the sun instead. This idea was very controversial at the time.

Fun Time

Q. Bob: How much do you think the moon is worth?
A. Maggie. One dollar, I guess, as it has four quarters.

Zhang Heng was a clever mathematician. He was very good with magic squares. Magic squares are numbers that add up to a common total when arranged in columns, rows, and diagonals.
He was not only a good mathematician, but he was also very good in literature and wrote beautiful poems.

Fun Time

Q. Why was the astronaut unable to reserve a room on the moon?
A. Because it was full.

Isaac Newton: Discovered Gravity

Isaac Newton is one of the most important and influential scientists of all time. He completely changed the way we look at and understand the world.

After watching an apple fall from a tree, he was inspired to develop the law of gravity. In his **gravitational theory**, he argued that all particles in the universe attract each other through gravity. Isaac Newton's laws of gravity help us understand how planets interact with other colliding **molecules** in the universe, how earthquakes ripple through the Earth's crust and how we can create buildings that are strong enough to withstand them.

Fun Time

Q. What do apple pies always say the day after Thanksgiving?
A. Good-pie to you all.

He also developed the three Laws of Motion that state that every object in the universe is in a state of motion. Although some of Isaac Newton's theories were replaced later by Albert Einstein's more accurate theories, they laid important groundwork for his work and other modern thoughts like relativity and physics.

Fun Time

Q. What do people find at the end of a rainbow?
A. "w".

Newton also invented the **Newtonian telescope**, which is still used widely today and was the first person who truly understood the rainbow and the concept of refracting light using a prism.

Fun Facts About Isaac Newton

1. He was a very secretive person. He was a very lonely person too. He never had any hobbies; he never married and trusted people enough to maintain a friendship. Many people believe that Isaac Newton could have kept some of his discoveries secret.

2. His mother wanted him to be a farmer, but he was passionate about science and mathematics, and he was determined to follow his dreams. He attended Trinity College and later went on to attend the University of Cambridge.

3. Newton was so obsessed with his research that he was not interested in his lecturing job at Cambridge. As a result, most students didn't attend his lectures. On many occasions, no one attended at all.

4. He quietly served in the parliament. He represented the University of Cambridge from 1689-1690. He spoke once throughout his service as a parliamentarian, apparently asking the user to close the window because it was too cold.

5. He had powerful academic rivalries. Most famous is his feud with German mathematician Gottfried Leibniz. They had disagreements about who invented calculus. Isaac Newton had invented his version and Gottfried Leibniz had invented and published his version. In the end, Isaac Newton was credited with inventing calculus, but Leibniz's version is the one that is frequently used today.

Ada Lovelace: Prophetess of the Computer Age

Ada Lovelace is popularly known as the **first computer programmer** in history. Her contribution to the world of science is celebrated on October 15th every year. On that day, women who have made a great impact in science and mathematics are also celebrated.

Fun Time

Tony: I am so smart. I can solve any math equation.
Jayne: How can you do that?
Tony: It's easy. You just multiply both sides by zero.

She was an expert at algorithms which refers to the step-by-step method of solving mathematical problems. Ada Lovelace wrote the first computer program for the Analytical Engine, which would become the present-day computer. She argued that this program could be used to calculate a series of complicated numbers, which are widely used in physics and mathematics.

Fun Time

Q. What did the two fours say when asked why they had skipped lunch?
A. Because we are already 8.

Percy Spencer: Invented the Microwave

Did you know that the invention of the **microwave** happened by accident? Unlike the 90% of American homes who use the microwave to heat their food daily, Percy Spencer was born into a poor family and often had to hunt his food.

Fun Time

A new computer software language was named Ada in 1979 in honor of her contribution to the field.

Percy Spencer worked at a company known as **Raytheon**, where hisjob was to develop microwave radars that could be used as**transmitters** during World War II. While he was visiting the labs, henoticed that the microwaves he was working on were melting thecandy bars in his pocket.

Surprised, Spencer sent out a boy to bring a package of popcorn.When he held it close to the microwaves, the popcorn exploded andfilled the room. He tr ied again with an uncooked egg inside a kettleand realized that he quickly had a fully-cooked egg.

Spencer quickly figured out that the waves could heat food if theycould be concentrated. So he created his first microwave, andpopcorns were the first food he cooked.

Fun Time

Q. What did baby corn say when mother corn asked himwhat he was doing?

A. He said he was looking for popcorn.

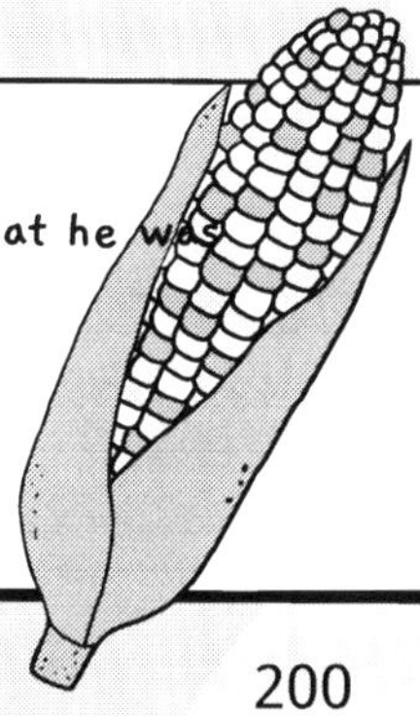

The sugar, water, and fats in food absorb the microwaves released by the oven and convert them to heat. Microwaves cook food evenly and quickly without using a lot of energy. However, most plastics, glass, and ceramics don't absorb microwaves. It was a luxury reserved for the rich back in the day.

Fun Time

Raytheon built the first microwave oven in 1947, and it was so huge – it weighed 750 pounds and was almost 6 feet tall. What's more, the first microwaves were very expensive. They were being sold at $5,000, which would be an equivalent of $52,000 today.

The Wright Brothers : Invented the Aeroplane

For centuries humans dreamt of flying like birds over the clouds. Lots of people tried and failed by trying to imitate the birds. That was until the Wright brothers solved this problem very creatively.

Fun Time

Alice: Maggie, Do you know what I always find odd?
Maggie: No, what?
Alice: Numbers cannot be divided by two.

For many years, experts in America and Europe tried to create a flying machine without success. Defying gravity was proving to be more difficult than any of them thought was possible. The Wright brothers would be the first people to successfully fly an airplane on Thursday, December 17th, 1903. Finally, the brothers seemed to find a formula that could work after so many failed attempts. As they grew up, Wilbur and Orville Wright were curious about flight. They studied and read everything they could find about flight, including other people's findings.

The biggest obstacle everyone faced was how to generate enough power to get the machine from the ground and sustain it in the air after it took off. The Wright brothers built a lightweight engine that could provide very high power than anything developed before. The successful flight of the first airplane resulted from years of dedication, persistence, determination, and work done continuously in secret.

Their invention revolutionized the world of transportation. Airplanes were going to make the world a very small place moving forward.

Fun Time

Teacher: Ben, are you sure the world is round?
Ben: Yes, and I will give you three reasons to prove it: my mom says so, my dad says so, and my sister says so.

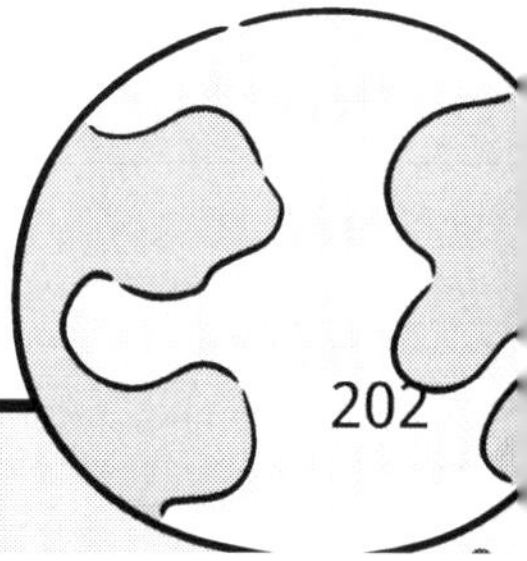

Put yourself in their shoes for a moment. Imagine yourself being told by everyone that your dream is impossible and that no one has ever done it before. How does it feel? Of course, it's very hard and discouraging. But what makes them keep going? The answer is that they believed in themselves. They were determined to learn whatever they didn't know. They keep imagining themselves living their dreams which makes them work hard to achieve them.

Hedy Lamar

If you don't know the person behind **Wi-Fi technology** and **Bluetooth**, it's time to thank the Hollywood actress Hedy Lamar, who was featured in films like "*Boom Town*" and "*Algiers*".

She made great contributions in the fields of systems, technology, and radio. For example, she invented a radio guidance system for torpedoes that was very helpful during World War II and laid the ground for developing Bluetooth and Wi-Fi.

Fun Time

Teacher: Does anyone know what the first English silent film was?
Student: If it was a silent film, no one would know if it was English or not.

Leonardo da Vinci

Leonardo da Vinci is probably the most famous and best known for his painting, **"Mona Lisa"**. For over 200 years, the Mona Lisa stayed hung in the Louvre gallery in Paris. But Leonardo da Vinci was not only a painting genius, but he was also an excellent poet, architect, inventor, scientist, composer, mathematician, and sculptor. He was a true genius and one of the most intelligent men who ever lived.

Put yourself in their shoes for a moment. Imagine yourself being told by everyone that your dream is impossible and that no one has ever done it before. How does it feel? Of course, it's very hard and discouraging. But what makes them keep going? The answer is that they believed in themselves. They were determined to learn whatever they didn't know. They keep imagining themselves living their dreams which makes them work hard to achieve them.

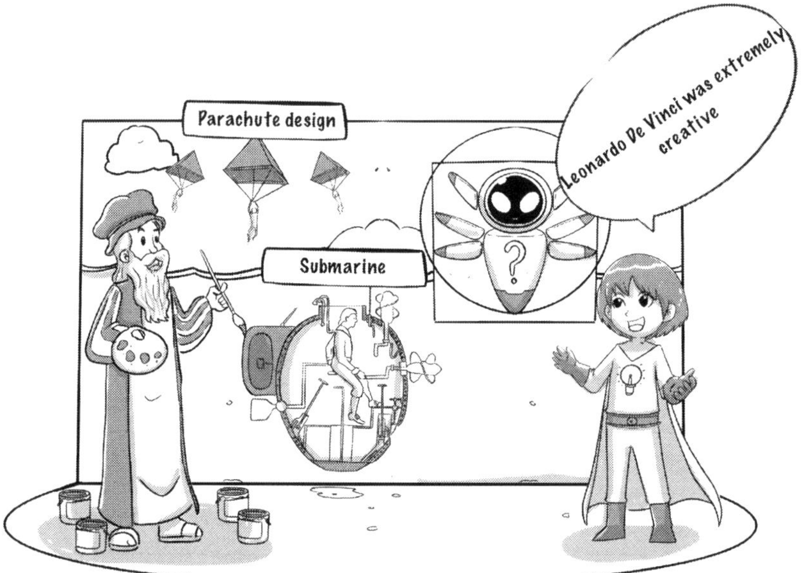

Fun Facts About Leonardo da Vinci

1. He loved animals so much that he decided to be a vegetarian. Being a vegetarian was very unusual in those days. He would buy animals from the market just to get home and set them free.

2. Leonardo was left-handed. Many people could not understand his notes because apart from being left-handed, he could write back to front, across the page, and from right to left. Many people believe that his style of writing was a way to keep his ideas secret.

3. Mona Lisa is the world's most famous painting. However, it was the painting of a Florentine official that Leonardo was asked to paint. Florence is an Italian city where Leonardo lived.

Fun Time

Robbie: Dad is complaining that his shaving brush has suddenly become hard.
Alex: That's strange! When I used it to paint our front door last night, it was soft.

4. He had a unique personality. In his later years, he would wear brightly colored clothes, long hair, and long beard down to his chest.

5. He might have become a super genius, but you would be intrigued to learn that he never set foot in school in his lifetime. He was homeschooled, and he quickly learned mathematics, reading, and writing.

Fun Time

Teacher: John, What can you do to make sure the school stays clean?
John: Stay at home, sir.

AMAZING KID INVENTORS

Kids are always smart, energetic, curious, and observant. They have an incredible sense of possibility and wonder. Most kids see the world as an endless and beautiful platform. When they are given an opportunity to let out their curiosity, they can achieve greatness.

You might, therefore, be surprised to find out that some of the most popular inventions you know today were born in the minds of children.

Let's explore them!

Fun Time

Q. How do popsicles leave their other popsicle friends?
A. They use a good by-sicle.

Frank Epperson: Invented the Popsicle

You are probably a great lover of **popsicles**, but did you know anEleven-year-old child invented it? In 1905, Frank Epperson was just playing outside the house with a concoction made of water and sodawater powder on winter's eve. The mixture was in a glass, and he was stirring it with a stick.

He forgot the mixture outside overnight, and it froze solid. So this is how the first popsicle came to be. The popsicle might have begun ona cold winter night in 1905, but it only gained popularity in 1922 when Frank Epperson offered it to people at a fireman's ball.

Frank Epperson was granted exclusive rights to the invention(patent) and called it "Eppsicle". He later changed the name to "popsicle" when his children started referring to it as such.

Fun Time

Q. Why are your fingers more reliable than any other part of the body?
A. They can always be counted on.

Louis Braille: Invented the Braille Code

It was so sad when Louis Braille caught an eye infection that left him blind at only three years old. Moving around became very difficult for him. He also tried to read by tracing his fingers over raised letters, but it was very challenging. However, as the old saying goes, "*Every cloud has a silver lining.*"

At 12 years old, he learned a silent method that the French military used for communication. He thought that if the process was simplified, it would help him read much better, which is exactly what he did. So he simplified the process and called it "Braille". In 1924, he first presented his work, and it was a huge success. Braille is used by the blind community all over the world today.

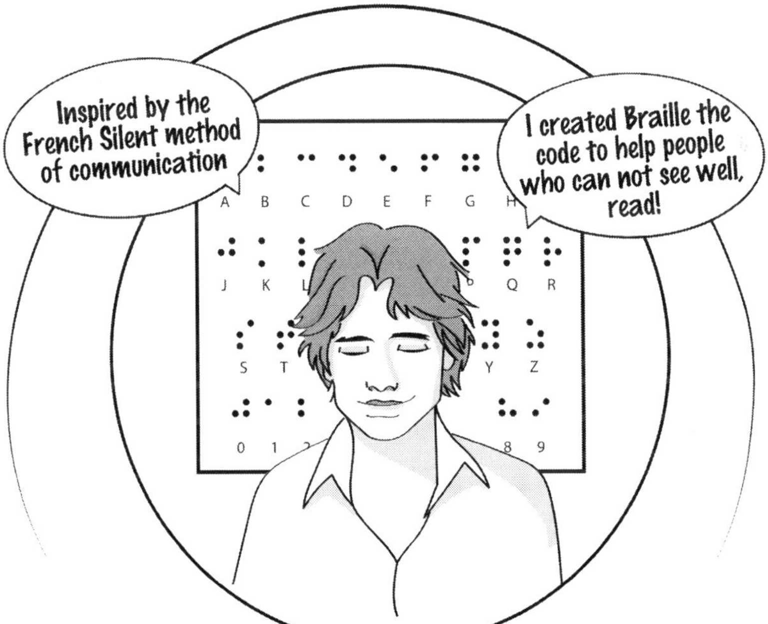

Fun Time

Q. What does Santa look for when he is a detective?
A. Santa clues

Albert Sadacca: Invented Christmas Lights

Candles were the only decorations people used to decorate their Christmas trees with before this invention. So it's ironic that people initially had more doubts about the safety of Christmas lights than open flames.

Slowly, the public started to come around and trust Christmas lights.However, the lights were very expensive at the time. That was until Albert, again, developed an affordable version of the Christmaslights.

His parents had a novelty lighting company, and Albert used it to produce the Christmas lights in 1925. Christmas lights have becomea common tradition ever since, thanks to this intelligent boy.

Fun Time

Q. Why did the Christmas tree have a problem standing up?
A. Because it didn't have any legs.

Fun Time

Q. What is it that we all do at the same time?
A. Grow older

George Nissen: Inventor of the Trampoline

Kids are very observant. One good example is: In 1930, a 16-year-old boy was watching trapeze artists perform. At the end of the performance, he saw that the artists had dropped into a net. George thought that if they had kept bouncing, the performance would have been more exciting and captivating.

He started working in his parent's garage, trying to come up with the invention. His first version of the trampoline had the canvas stretched over a metal frame. Then, when he was older, he perfected his art using a nylon canvas to give the trampoline more bounce.

Fun Time

Q. What does everyone have that goes up but will never come back?
A. An age

Philo T Farnsworth

While many 15-year-olds would rather spend most of their time watching TV, Philo T Farnsworth was busy trying to invent it at the same age.

Farnsworth was born in 1906, and by the time he was a teenager, he had created many sketches of instruments that could contribute to the invention of the television in significant ways. His works, later on, contributed a lot to the invention of TV. His most famous invention would be the first video tube camera, otherwise known as 'image dissector' (it's like the gun that shoots images to the screen of the old TVs)

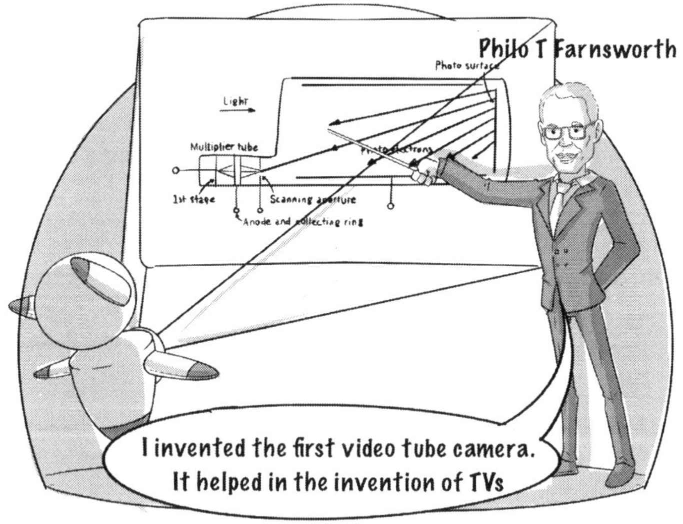

Fun Time

He was the inspiration behind the popular movie Futurama's Professor Farnsworth.

Cassidy Goldstein: Invented Crayon Holders

You've probably experienced this too; you are almost done with your greatest picture of the day – a beautiful boat sailing across the blue ocean when suddenly your crayon breaks off, leaving you with no other choice but to quit. But, I mean, what's a budding artist to do?

Well, Cassidy Goldstein wasn't one to surrender easily. In 1999, she was faced with packets full of worn-out crayons that she didn't know what to do with. So she went out in search of something that could extend their life. She found a tube used for holding fresh flowers, and the crayons fit in perfectly. As a result, she was able to continue her coloring till the very end.

She was given exclusive rights to the invention later on. The crayon holders can be found in most toy shops across the US. Her invention also won her the award for "*Youth Inventor of The Year.*"

Fun Time

Bella: I have a crayon that looks so much like a strawberry.
Maisie: What do you call it?
Bella: A cranberry.

Fun Time

Q: Why was the little girl unhappy with her unexpected box of crayons?
A: Because it was out of the blue.

Ben Franklin: Invented the Swim Flippers

Ben Franklin was a high achiever as an adult; he was one of the founding fathers of the United States, political philosopher, writer, diplomat, statesman, among others. He was a jack of all trades, no doubt, but did you know he was also a child inventor?

As an 11-year-old in the early 1700, he figured out that he would swim better and move swiftly in the water if he had more surface area to use for pushing. His first design featured handheld fins created out of oval-shaped planks with holes left in the middle to hold his hands and feet.

Fun Time

Jayne: I have a new Barbie that lives underwater.
Betty: What is it called?
Jayne: Doll fin

Fun Facts About Ben Franklin

1. Many people consider him the most intelligent American, but you might be surprised to learn that he had only two years of formal education. He attended the Boston Latin School for only two years, then dropped out and joined his family's candle and soap-making business.

2. He invented a musical instrument cal led "**glass armonica**" . The harmonica was very popular . Some of the most successful musicians in history, such as Beethoven and Mozart, used it to compose music.

3. He loved swimming so much so that his participation and contribution to the sport earned him a position in the **International Swimming Hall of Fame**.

Fun Time

Q. Why did sports stadiums never get hot?
A. They are always full of fans.

4. He found success as a teenage writer. He wrote about fashion, religion, women's rights, and even marriage.

5. He spent more than 42 years of his life studying science. He went on to invent the lightning rod, heating stove, and bifocal glasses.

Fun Time

Mom: Marie, you need to eat your carrots. They are good for your eyes.
Marie: How do you know that, mommy?
Mom: Well, have you ever seen a rabbit wearing glasses?

Param Jaggi: Invented the Algae Mobile

The spirit of invention didn't die with the older generation. Param Jaggi was already working with inventors when he was just 13 years old. As he was learning, he thought about the possibility of creating a device that could convert the **carbon dioxide** that cars produce to oxygen. So he went on to create just that, and he called it the **Algae Mobile**.

He patented his invention in 2011 and won multiple awards for it. Experts agree that Param's invention will one day revolutionize our world's air quality and reduce **air pollution** significantly.
Recently Param Jaggi was featured in Forbes' 30 under 30 lists of most promising innovators that have contributed greatly to the energy sector.

Chester Greenwood: Invented Earmuffs

Chester Greenwood, a 15-year-old child, was playing outside in the cold winter season of 1873. He soon started shivering, and his ears became painfully cold as he was ice-skating. He wrapped a scarf around his head but quickly realized that it didn't help much. So he started thinking of a better solution.

He created a wireframe and asked his grandmother to sew beaver skins into it. This would be the world's first earmuffs.

He even sold the earmuffs to soldiers during World War I and patented his invention when he was only 19

Fun Time

My friend John has fantastic hearing. He's a real super-ear-o!

Catherine Wong

Not all countries have basic medicalinstruments for everyone. Catherine Wong, a 17-year-old girl, thought about using current smartphones that almost everyone has to cover some basic medical exams.

She thought it was probably a good idea to invent a tiny device that could show a patient's heartbeat on their phone screens. Patients can check for any kind of problems using the device and seek medical help accordingly. So she invented an electrocardiogram that transmits real-time medical data through cell phones.

Catherine Wong's invention can improve healthcare for millions of people all over the world.

Fun Time

I have a cousin who studied cardiology for seven years but didn't get hisdegree. Do you know what his father calls him?

A heart failure.

FINAL THOUGHTS

Being an inventor or scientist is just a title. We don't need to havemultiple years of experience in one domain to become inventors. Wejust need to cont inue being curious and never stop asking questions,even though they may sound silly.

If there is one thing very young kids like to do frequently, it is askingquestions. They are very observant and curious. They are alwaysasking questions like, what does it mean? Or, why does that happen?What is this used for? Some of them may sound silly. For example,why is it that ants don't get lost and find their way home? But if youtry to find the answer and keep doing research, you may come upwith a new form of a problem-solving technique called "ant colonyalgorithm," which is used in computer science and mathematics.

The fact is we are born scientists, and we just need to remain one.Asking questions and seeking answers is how we explore and expand our knowledge. So keep an open mind over the answers and different possibilities of solutions, even though they may sound silly. Always consider all the possible answers and solutions, then filter them one by one based on feasibility and consultations with others (parents or your teachers or specialists).

Remember Albert Einstein's quote: "*I am neither especially clever nor especially gifted. I am only very, very curious*". You don't have to be
an adult to have amazing thoughts and ideas and put them into use.
The kid inventors in this list found brilliant ideas about solving common, everyday problems and making life more interesting. Other interesting inventions by kids include snowmobiles, water skis, Superman, and toy trucks. This list is by no means exhaustive, both for the kid inventors and famous philosophers. Many inventions are still in the works, and there is always room for more.

Jokes About Inventors

Teacher: Alex, what can you tell me about the inventor of the light bulb?Alex: He had a bright future, miss.

Q. What did the inventor of suspenders win?
A: The Nobelt Prize.

Q. Has anyone heard of an Italian painter and inventor who did not likeChristmas?
A: His name was Leonardo da Grinchi.

When the invertor of the air conditioner died, the funeral was a huge event.Thousands of fans attended it.

The person who invented the umbrella was a little indecisive. Originally itwas just going to be a brella, but he wasn't sure, and it indeed up as anummm brella.

CHAPTER 9: FUN FACTS TO SHARE WITH YOUR FRIENDS

1. Did you know that the heir to the British throne, **Prince Charles** has a car fueled by wine? This approach is very entertaining, but the future king of England has an Aston Martin modified to use wine as its primary fuel.

2. Kids ask an average of 3,00 questions every day. However, a UK study in 2013 revealed that parents could answer up to 300 kids' questions every day, or a single question after every 2 ½ minutes. The parents in the study reported that the hardest questions asked by kids were, "What trees grow upward?" and "why we don't walk on our hands?"

Fun Time

Q. Everyone has something they cannot lose. What is it?
A. Their shadow

3. Escaping prison is legal in Mexico. Germany, Austria, and several other countries agree on this fun fact as well. In these countries, escaping prison is viewed as a natural human act rather than a crime. But, of course, they will go looking for you and put you back in jail if you escape.

4. Do you know the full name of Los Angeles? It is "**El Pueblo de Nuestra Señora la Reina de los Angeles de Porciuncula.**" That's quite a mouthful!

5. Martin Luther King Junior and Anne Frank were both born in the same year. Anne Frank is famously known and associated with the Nazi brutalities that happened in **World War II**. At the same time, Martin Luther King Junior symbolized the civil rights movement and equality in the '60s. These two events seem like they happened so far apart, but these two famous historical figures were born in 1929 – Anne Frank on June 12th, Martin Luther King Junior on January 15th.

6. Studies show that it takes most people seven minutes at most to fall asleep. If you want to fall asleep faster, you can remember or review a nice dream you've dreamt before.

Fun Time

Q. How can you make the number seven even?
A. Simply remove the letter 's'.

7. Did you know that the US government sets an official plan for a Zombie Apocalypse? The US government wants to be prepared for a real-life version of The Walking Dead. So in 2011, the American government designed a 31-page plan called CONPLAN 8888-11 (Counter-Zombie Dominance Plan) if a zombie apocalypse happens.

8. The only country in the world with no official capital city is called **Nauru**. Nauru is a tiny Pacific Island nation whose government offices are located in the Yaren District. It is a district that is close to the airport.

9. Before Abraham Lincoln became the 16th President of the United States, he was a very successful professional wrestler.

10. You can figure out what the weather will be by counting a cricket's chirps.

11. Did you know that slugs have four noses and caterpillars have 12 eyes? Sounds excessive, but these features are usually necessary.

12. When you shake ketchup, it becomes 1,000 times thinner. In addition, when ketchup is shaken, the spherical tomato particles inside become thinner ellipses making the ketchup thinner.

13. The **Antarctic Polar** is the largest desert in the world, and it is covered in snow. The Sahara Desert is huge, at 3.5 million square miles, but it doesn't compare to this icy desert. At 5.5 million square miles, the Antarctic Polar desert is a true monster covering the whole continent of Antarctica.

    The simple definition of a desert is a place that receives less than 10 inches of moisture in a year, and it doesn't have to be hot.

14. You end up with three kidneys after a kidney transplant. Kidney transplants are very common, but did you know that surgeons always leave the diseased kidney intact? The new kidney is placed on the front side of the body in the lower belly area.

15. Human blood is as salty as the water in the seas and the oceans.

Fun Time

Teacher: Sam, why are you looking at a blood bank in my class?
Sam: Because my mother says I have a blood test tomorrow, sir.

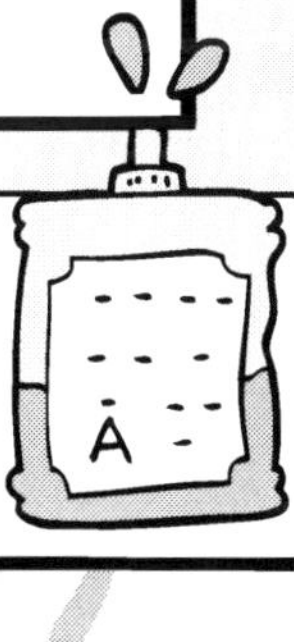

16. Do you know the approximate number of cells in the human body? It's around a very huge number of 100 trillion cells.

17. Hippos, large as they may be, can run faster than human beings. Never underestimate them because of their massive size.

18. Like fingerprints in human beings, the nose prints in a dog's nose are unique to each dog.

19. The game of monopoly has been played with over 480 million people in the world.

20. High-heeled shoes were first designed for wealthy men. The high-heeled trend has been associated with femininity for as long as most of us can remember then; it's a little odd to think that Persians invented the high-heeled shoes in the 10th century as a luxury reserved for wealthy men. Women took over this trend in the 18th century and have never looked back.

Fun Time

Q. What did the burglar put on before entering someone' s house?
A. Sneakers

21. A new study found out that more twins are being born now than ever before. The "twinning rate," as experts popularly refer to it, has increased by 1/3 since the '80s. So in every 1,000 births, three instead, the more twins are being born, which translates to 1.6 million twins born every year.

22. According to research done by the United Nations, every year, approximately 1.3 billion metric tons of food are wasted worldwide. Of the food wasted, 61% comes from homes, 13% from grocery stores, and 26% from restaurants and other food services. 822 million people suffer from undernourishment. Statistically, a child dies from hunger every 10 seconds.

23. Did you know that when a sea slug's head is cut off, it can grow a whole new body again? Experts at the Nara Women's University in Japan observed that the sea slug, Elysia cf. marginalia, increased back its body, the heart included, after 20 days.

24. Out of every three emails sent out, almost one of them is spam. Up to now, 45% of all email traffic is made up of spam. You've probably sent hundreds of them yourself.

25. Did you know that pineapples are a natural meat tenderizer? Because pineapples have a lot of bromelain enzymes, they can break down complex chains of proteins in meat and make it tender. However, the bromelain in pineapple is so powerful that it could eat away at the skin over time and leave sores on the skin. For this reason, pineapple processors are expected to wear protective gear such as gloves and goggles at all times.

26. One of the oldest jobs of all is dentistry. It has been around for as long as human beings existed and had teeth. In addition, scientists have found evidence of teeth drilling using prehistoric tools dating back thousands of years.

Fun Time

Q: When is an apple not an apple?
A: When it is a pineapple.

27. When you are on a flight, you lose up to 30% of your tastebuds sensitivity. Maybe this explains why the food served inan airplane is usually bad. A study done by the *Fraunhofer Institute for Building Physics* in Germany reports that thesensitivity of a person's taste buds can be reducedsignificantly by the low pressure and high elevation duringflights.

28. There are only two animals in the world that love spicy food:human beings and the tree shrew. However, new researchhas found that these adorable animals enjoy spiced cornpellets while other mammals avoid them altogether.

29. Did you know that a dentist invented cotton candies? Noone knows if the dentist, known as William Morrison, hadother mot ives when he invented this sweet confection. Still,he made sure other dentists had many patients visiting theirclinics every year, especially kids.

30. The word "Set" is an English word with the highest number ofdefinit ions. The *Guinness Book of World Records* reportsthat the "set" has 430 different definitions listed in the*Oxford English Dictionary, 2nd Edition*. 60,000 words and326,000 characters are used to define all the different meanings.

31. Pigeons can differentiate paintings done by either Picasso orMonet. The *Journal of Experimental Analysis of Behavior* published a study in 1995 that highlighted the ability ofpigeons to tell the difference between paintings done bythese two famous painters. Furthermore, even when the paintngs were inverted, the pigeons could still tell themapart.

32. Maria Paraskeva set the world record for the longest wedding veil that ever existed. The veil was stretched 22,843feet or as long as 63.5 football fields combined.

Fun Time

Q. Where did the footballers visit when they wanted to dance?
A. A football.

33. Did you know that Pringles are not potato chips, as many people believe? If you come across a can of pringles, study the ingredients carefully. You will see no indication of "chips" anywhere on the packaging. That's because pringles are made of potato flakes that have been dehydrated and pressed into that familiar parabolic shape. Even the *Food and Drug Administration* banned the company from advertising the product as "potato chip," and that's why they settled for "potato crisp."

Fun Time

Bill: I once saw a potato with right angles.
Ted: Would that still be called a potato?
Bill: No, I think it is called a square root.

34. Showers are known to improve a person's creativity. In 2012, the *Psychological Science* journal published a study that showed that when your mind wonders, just like it does when you are in the shower, you are more likely to solve complex creativity problems.

Fun Time

Q. What do you find in the middle of a coconut?
A. The letter 'o'.

35. Water makes different splashing sounds at different temperatures. The sound produced by cold water and hot water differs slightly when it is being poured. This is because heat changes the viscosity or the thickness of the water, which then varies the pitch when it is run. Being that cold water is thicker, it makes a pouring sound that is high-pitched.

Fun Time

Husband to friend: I have no idea why my wife bought some coconut shampoo yesterday. We do not have any coconuts in our house.

36. Falling coconuts are very dangerous. They kill more people than sharks do. Sharks have a very bad reputation for killing people violently, but as humble as they may seem, falling coconuts are to be feared more. Every year 150 people lose their lives when a falling coconut hits them. That's way less compared to the ten people sharks kill every year.

37. The state of Wyoming, in the US, has only two escalators. The two escalators are found in banks. Wyoming has very few inhabitants. It is sparsely populated. The population of cows outnumbers that of people by far. There are about 580,000 people and 1.3 million cows in the state.

Fun Time

Q. What is the same size as a cow but is weightless?
A. The cow' s shadow.

38. Less than 20% of laughter is a result of funny jokes and stories. Robert Provine, an expert scientist, suggests that most laughter isn't a result of humor. Instead, most laughter is simply a response to regular statements and conversations. The good thing is that the laughter, however short, helps to build stronger bonds among people. People who laugh together become closer.

39. Did you know that dogs can understand some words in the English vocabulary? If trained well, dogs can understand approximately 165 words. They respond best and faster to words with hard consonants such as "t" and "r". Maybe this could explain why they can hear the word "treat" from miles away.

Fun Time

Boy: Mom, what can I have for breakfast?
Mom: Anything you like except lunch and dinner.

40. Have you ever heard of the rumor that starts on the internet from time to time saying that natural redheads will become extinct by the year 2060? Rest easy if you are a redhead because this is only a myth. Redheads are always going to be born, as rare as they are.

41. Koalas have fingerprints. Even more fascinating is the fact that koala prints have lots of similarities to human fingerprints. Crime scene investigators totally agree with this fact.

42. Rolls-Royce makes the most expensive cars in the world. The name of the car is Rolls-Royce Sweptail with a market price of about $13 million. What's more, even if you were that rich, you wouldn't be able to buy it. That's because this car was built for a specific customer who has to pass some qualifications to own it.

Fun Time

Q. What did the police say when they found someone had stolen the wheels off their police car?

A. We will work tirelessly to find the culprit.

43. You are familiar with police dogs but have you ever seen police geese? Well, it turns out that police in a remote partof China uses geese guards. As you probably know, geese can stay alert for long and cause loud noises and commotion when disturbed. The Dongwan police in China aretaking advantage of this factor, and they are even claimingthat the geese have already stopped more than one theft sofar.

Fun Time

Q. Why do the police enjoy playing baseball?
A. It allows them to get a catch.

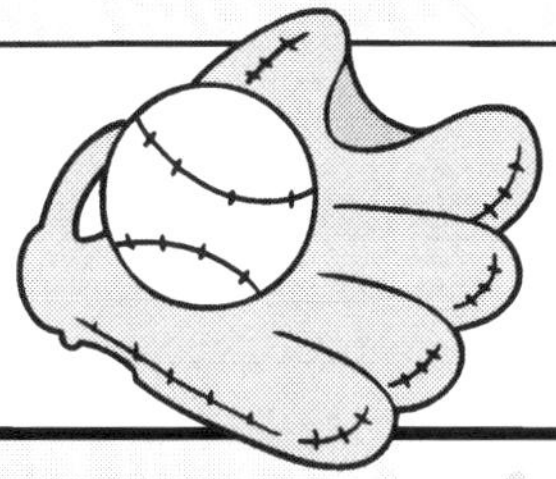

Fun Time

Q. Where would spaghetti go if it wanted to dance?
A. To a meatball.

44. Twins are more likely to be born in Benin, a country in Central Africa, than in any other country in the world. The average twin birth rate in the world is just 13 twins/1,000 births, but Benin has more than double this rate of twins. The twinning rate in Benin is around 30twins/1,000 births. Factors like diet and genetics can contribute to this phenomenon.

45. Did you know that spaghetti is a plural noun? The singular form of spaghetti is **spaghetto**. Can you guess what thesingular form of confetti and graffiti is? Confetto and graffito

46. Did you know that the song Mary had a little lamb is based on a true story? Mary Sawyer was an 11-year-old girl fromBoston. Her pet followed her to school one day. She loved her pet dearly, and she, later on, sold wool from it to raise money for an old church in her hometown.

47. It's a little funny, but a pig was executed for attacking a child in ancient France. The pig was arrested by officials, lockedup in jail, sent to court, faced a trial for murder chargeswhere it was found guilty and then sentenced to executionby hanging.

Fun Time

Mike: Did you enjoy the joke that the boxer told you?
Millie: Yes, especially the punchline.

48. The **Anglo-Zanzibar** war is popularly known as the shortest war in history. It lasted only 38 minutes! It was over before it even started. The war was between Zanzibar and Br i tain. Zanzibar surrendered, and Britain won.

49. Did you know that the game **Tug of War** was a famous Olympic game? Britain was very good at it and they went on to win five gold medals.